This Superior Place

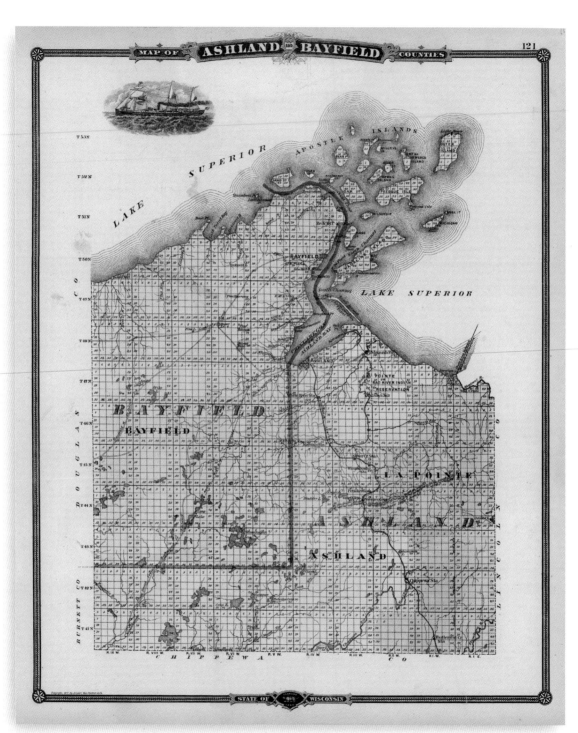

Map from 1878 detailing Ashland and Bayfield

WHi Image ID 73680

THIS SUPERIOR PLACE

Stories of Bayfield and the Apostle Islands

DENNIS McCANN

Wisconsin Historical Society Press

Published by the Wisconsin Historical Society Press
Publishers since 1855

© 2013 by the State Historical Society of Wisconsin

Publication of this book was made possible in part by a grant from the Amy Louise Hunter fellowship fund.

wisconsin**history**.org

Printed in Wisconsin, USA
Cover design by Brian Donahue / bedesign, inc.
Interior design and typesetting by Brad Norr Design
17 16 15 14 13   1 2 3 4 5

Front cover: Bayfield's waterfront, 2011. Photo by Grandon Harris.
Back cover: Bayfield's bustling waterfront at the turn of the twentieth century. Photo courtesy of the Bayfield Heritage Association, 2005-194-006.

Library of Congress Cataloging-in-Publication Data
McCann, Dennis, 1950— This superior place : stories of Bayfield and the Apostle Islands / Dennis McCann.
     pages cm
  Includes bibliographical references and index.
  ISBN 978-0-87020-579-8 (paperback : alkaline paper) 1. Bayfield (Wis.)—Description and travel. 2. Bayfield (Wis.)—History. 3. Bayfield (Wis.)—History—Anecdotes. 4. Apostle Islands (Wis.)—Description and travel. 5. Apostle Islands (Wis.)—History. 6. Apostle Islands (Wis.)—History—Anecdotes. I. Title.
  F589.B3M35 2013
  977.5'13—dc23
                              2012039455

To Barb, as always
And to Judy,
for bringing us to this special place

Preface

H alf a lifetime ago—we debate the exact year but have narrowed it down to 1981 or '82—my wife and I first made the long drive from southern Wisconsin to the state's northern rim and the shore of Lake Superior. We checked into a room we had reserved at late notice and soon after caught the ferry to Madeline Island, where we met a friend who was staying at what was then the elegantly rustic Chateau Madeleine. Judy was dining on the Chateau's pier, so we joined her for a glass of wine and our first glorious Lake Superior sunset, a beautiful event even before the disappearing sun graced the horizon with a brilliant pink-orange blush atop the mainland's dark green forests.

If we didn't expressly say "Where has this been all our lives?" we certainly felt it. The next morning we checked out of our cabin in Bayfield, crossed again to La Pointe, and checked into an odd little round house on the main street (it would later become a coin-operated laundry), which came with a balcony that afforded us a bird's-eye view of the passing tourists.

And so it began. We returned the next year, and the year after that. And when we saw our first Madeline Island Fourth of July parade, an old-fashioned bit of red, white, and blue Americana that ends with speeches and songs at the historic Madeline Island Museum, an island Fourth became as much a part of our lives as Christmas or Easter. We have missed only one parade since that first one, and while the parade has grown and gone a bit island upscale—you can still decorate your kids or your dog and march proudly down the street, but now there are floats and more units and sometimes flying hot dogs—its original charm has hardly been gentrified.

It wasn't long before one long slog up the belly of the state each year wasn't enough; we started squeezing in an extra visit, or even three in a year. It helped that, as a traveling newspaper columnist, I could usually find stories that contained critically important news for readers who lived 375 miles south in Milwaukee, even if many didn't understand that Madeline was the island in Lake Superior, not the one off the tip of Door County—but no matter. Have company car, will travel to Madeline.

When we began visiting Bayfield in winter it was just further evidence, as if any was needed, that this special place had gotten a hold on us, that it had become what one friend who similarly loves Lake Superior calls "soul country." Heart and soul, as it turned out. In 1998 we bought a piece of property just south of Bayfield and later built a home that looks at La Pointe and Madeline Island across often-shimmering Chequamegon Bay.

Some might say, well, it took you long enough. And that's true. In most communities popular with tourists, T-shirts or sweatshirts are souvenirs enough, but there are many stories of visitors who came to Bayfield for the first time on a Friday and left on Sunday owning a second home.

It can be that kind of place.

All of that is meant merely as full disclosure that the book you are holding is hardly a dispassionate telling of the story of Bayfield and the Apostle Islands. I am not a historian but rather a newspaperman by training, though my professional duties often involved sharing stories about Wisconsin history. What this is, then, at least by intention, is an effort to share the events that made Bayfield, and its environs, what it is today—a community where the past was layered with good times and down times, where natural beauty was the one resource that could not be exhausted by the hand of man, and where history is ever present.

That is not to suggest Bayfield has not changed in its more than 150 years as a city, because change has been a constant part of life here. Industries have come and gone; hopes have been raised and sometimes dashed. While old family names continue generation by generation, newcomers have arrived to spend their retirement years or, ever optimistic, to start new businesses. This community built on hard work on land and on water is now more dependent than ever before on offering recreation and relaxation.

At the same time, reminders of the past are everywhere.

The onetime cooperage for the Booth fishing company near the ferry landing on Bayfield's harbor front, once a launching point for fleets of fishing boats, now houses a kayak business for paddlers heading out on the big lake.

The sprawling Chateau Boutin, the lakefront home built by the son of a lumberman and fisherman, is now an inn for Bayfield visitors, its beautiful curved leaded-glass windows and ornate woodwork elegant reminders of another time.

The old Bayfield County Courthouse, orphaned when the upstart city of Washburn stole the county seat in 1892, now houses the headquarters of the Apostle Islands National Lakeshore, a duty every bit as important as housing courtrooms and real estate records.

And in downtown Bayfield, the longtime bank building on the corner of Rittenhouse and Second Avenue—built of locally quarried Lake Superior brownstone—still bears the chiseled name of R. D. Pike, one of the city's biggest movers and shakers in pioneer days. Among his other accomplishments, Pike founded the local telephone company, brought electric streetlights to town, and owned the "Little Daisy" sawmill that was once one of the most productive mills in the North.

It was Pike who moved an early newspaper editor to note, "Bayfield is emphatically a fish town. No wonder, when it is remembered that the most prominent citizen there is a Pike."

The building with Pike's name attached is now in the business of selling T-shirts and sweatshirts to visitors. Bayfield today is emphatically a tourist town.

But a hometown, as well, to both longtime residents and the more recently arrived, with all of the civic issues communities everywhere face, from school funding to providing family-supporting jobs in a mostly seasonal economy, yet without letting new development mar the natural beauty that is the ultimate draw.

Bayfield's first library was established as a free reading room in 1857. Philanthropist Andrew Carnegie provided $10,000 to the Bayfield Library Board, and architect Henry Wildhagen designed the Greek Revival-style building with the striking Ionic columns of locally quarried brownstone. The Bayfield Carnegie Library opened its doors January 10, 1904.

Courtesy of the Bayfield Heritage Association, 1980-49-064

And while it is fine for a passing newspaperman to pronounce Bayfield and the Apostle Islands "paradise," as a *Chicago Tribune* writer did some years back, such a lofty title can hardly erase the problems and challenges—some peculiar to this northerly place—such as black bears that do not respect "Closed" signs on sweet-smelling bakeries, an ice road pocked with cracks and soft spots that too often fails to give resident islanders the freedom to cross at will, and, some years most of all, balky springs that refuse to follow the dictates of the Gregorian calendar, the phases of the moon, or the urgent pleadings of winter-weary residents.

Still, let summer come and warm the blue water of Chequamegon Bay, let the bright sun dance on the surface of the water while sailboats ride the breezes, and this is still the place that prompted the earliest recorded visitors to comment on its winsome ways. It is, then and now, a superior place.

No book is a singular accomplishment, of course, and so I owe my thanks to more people than I can probably recall, but I'll try.

The idea for this book came from Demaris Brinton at Apostle Islands Booksellers, and what book writer can turn down a bookseller with lofty goals? I am honored again by the willingness of Kathy Borkowski, director of the Wisconsin Historical Society Press, to take on another of my projects, and to all on the staff at that great institution, especially my editor, Barbara Walsh, who helped to turn pages of words into an actual book.

In Bayfield, gratitude goes out to all those who were here long before I began paying attention and who so willingly shared their memories of times gone by. Thanks also to Bob Mackreth, who well knows the human history of the Apostle Islands, for sharing stories that he has collected. For invaluable assistance and access to their fascinating photo archives, I thank Bill Gover and Gary Gaynor of the Bayfield Heritage Association as well as David Cooper, Neil Howk, and Damon Panek of the Apostle Islands National Lakeshore/National Park Service. Steve Cotherman and Sheree Peterson of the Madeline Island Museum provided fact-checking expertise. And special appreciation must be given Roberta Menger and Theresa Weber at the Bayfield Carnegie Library, a true civic treasure, for coming up with everything my inquiring heart could ask, and for further stretching what might already be the most lenient overdue policies in librarydom.

This Superior Place

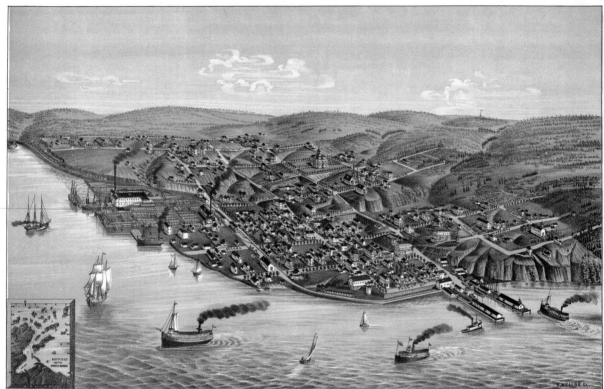

F. WELLGE SK.

COPYRIGHTED & PUBLISHED BY NORRIS, WELLGE & CO. N? 205 SECOND ST. MILWAUKEE WIS.

BECK & PAULI, Litho, Milwaukee, Wis

BIRDS EYE VIEW OF

BAYFIELD, WIS.

COUNTY SEAT OF BAYFIELD COUNTY.

1886

1 The Island View Hotel, N. P. Willey & Son, Prop's
3 J. H. Monroe, Dry Goods, Shoes, Clothing, Provisions, Etc
4 Wm. Hankins, Groceries and Provisions and Meat Market
5 Andrew Tate, Drugs and Medicines.
6 N. Boutin, General Store.
7 La Bonte House, N. La Bonte, Prop.
8 C. T. Andreas, Jeweler, L. S. Specimens and News Depot
9 D. Allen Pratt, Furniture and Undertaking.
10 D. J. Etsell, Hardware.
11 Erwin Leihy, General Merchandise.
12 Harlow City House and Livery, H. R. Lindsey, Prop.
13 German House, George A. Stahl, Prop.
14 Boutin & Mahan, General Merchandise and Wholesale
   (Fish Dealers.—N. Boutin, Postmaster.

A County Court House.
B Episcopal Church.
C Methodist   "
D Catholic   "
E New School House.
G School House.
H Catholic School.
K Convent.

L U. S. Land Office.
T Town Hall.
P Pikes Saw Mill,—Planing Mill,—Docks,
   Office Capt. R. D. Pike, Prop.
R R. R. Depot, C. St. P. M. & O. R. R.
N Bayfield County Press, Currie G. Bell, Prop.
V Dalrymple Dock,

15 Fred. Fischer, General Merchandise.
16 Robert Inglis, Gen'l Ticket Office and Insurance.
17 William Herbert, Harlow City Saloon.
18 Cream City House, L. Bachand, Prop.
19 Miss Nellie Tyler, Millinery and Fancy Goods.
20 John Stuart, Groceries and Provisions.
21 Lake View House, J. P. Horsley, Prop.
22 Union House, S. Boutin, Prop.
23 A. C. Hayward, General Merch. and Indian Curios.
24 Dr. H. Hannum, M. D. Res., Office at Tate's Drug Store
25 James Chapman, General Merchandise.
   La Pointe: Madelaine Island, The oldest
   Trading Point in the Northwest
   Settled in 1867.

1 In the Beginning

Its name suggests a glorious meeting of verdant farms and that famously shining Big-Sea-Water, and it is certainly true that orchard-blessed little Bayfield has gazed from Wisconsin's northern rim into the blue waters of Lake Superior's Chequamegon Bay since its founding in 1856.

In fact, though, Bayfield was christened not for its sublime setting but after an admiral, Henry W. Bayfield of the British Navy, fitting enough for a community whose founders dreamed would become a port city the world would notice, and that today is still visited by thousands of sailors, boaters, paddlers, and lake lovers every year. Three decades before the new town was platted and the first log cabin was erected, Henry Bayfield—not yet an admiral but a young naval officer—visited the region while performing the first surveys of Lake Superior.

Let other communities take their names from natural resources or prominent politicians; Bayfield's name was linked to the greatest of the Great Lakes by his direct experience with it, the same way the city and its people have always been connected to the lake. The following spring, Henry Bayfield wrote to Henry M. Rice, the city's founder, to express his pleasure at being so honored.

"I little thought when encamping there among the Indians 33 years ago that my tent was pitched near the site of a future town that was to bear my name," Bayfield wrote. "I trust that you will believe me to be very much gratified by this mark of your kind consideration and appreciation of my labors in those times and that you will accept my sincere thanks with every good wish for the prosperity of your town."

If Henry Bayfield had not imagined a town on that site, Henry Mower Rice certainly had. A member of the Minnesota territorial legislature, former fur trader, and later land developer, Rice was granted a patent in 1855 on 349 acres on the mainland directly across the bay from the fur-trade community of La Pointe. He envisioned a

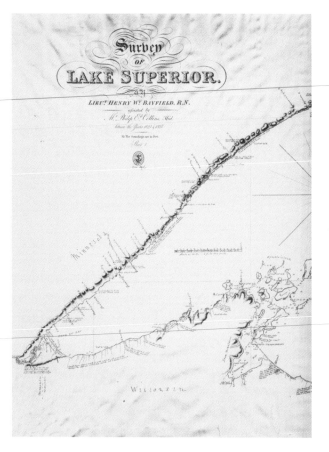

Survey of Lake Superior including Wisconsin and Minnesota, 1825, created by Henry Bayfield

WHi Image ID 49143

port city that could rival Superior or even Chicago in prominence and commerce, and other investors—including some from as far away as Washington, DC—shared the dream sufficiently to invest in his Bayfield Land Company. Surveyors were hired, streets were platted, trees were felled, and the first cabin was built in March 1856.

Of course, Bayfield's earliest settlers were hardly the first to find their way to the Chequamegon region, the area that included Chequamegon Bay, the Bayfield peninsula, and the twenty-two Apostle Islands. Native Americans were present in the area thousands of years before the first Europeans arrived in the seventeenth century. When French explorers established outposts on Madeline Island, the largest of the Apostles, and made the island a key site in the North American fur trade, they shared it with the Ojibwe, the dominant tribe at that time, who considered Madeline a spiritual as well as physical home. After the Treaty of 1854, the Ojibwe were relocated from Madeline Island to reservations at Red Cliff, three miles from the future Bayfield town site, and at Odanah on the Bad River, while the village of La Pointe began reinventing itself for the post–fur trade era.

Still, Bayfield was by any definition a frontier city, and its earliest residents, if not the first in the region, were classic pioneers, daring and determined to make new lives by taming the wilderness on the shores of the beautiful but often harsh big lake. By the time it celebrated its first birthday in 1857, the city of Bayfield had some 100 buildings and 112 residents.

More of both, of course, would be needed if Bayfield was to take its place among Wisconsin's vibrant new communities, so as one of its first acts the young city of Bayfield turned quickly to luring more settlers. Its location on the shore of Lake Superior in far northern Wisconsin offered an area rich in resources, but the site was also remote and sparsely populated, so in the manner popular in the mid-nineteenth century Bayfield published a "come one, come all" guide aimed at settlers, immigrants, and prospective business owners.

The document might be viewed today as more a carnival barker come-on than as totally factual guide to the region's assets, so exaggerated were its boasts. But accentuating the positive has always been the first step in sales, from Fuller's brushes to heal-all

patent medicines, and selling itself to interested parties was the nascent city's overriding goal. It was no occasion for modesty. "Please read and circulate!" read the plea titled "Bayfield, Lake Superior," which promised to touch on the city's early history, situation, harbor, mineral and agricultural resources, railroads and stage road, lumber, fisheries, climate, and more.

And, lest any prospective settler miss the point, the cover added, "An account of a pleasure tour to Lake Superior."

In the florid style of the day, the unknown author began with a bow to the first non-natives to come to the country bordering the Great Lakes, the French missionaries and Canadian voyageurs who were lured not by the "thirst of sordid gain" but rather the "spirit of religious enthusiasm."

"Kissing the symbol of their faith, and with the 'Te Deum laudamus' issuing from their parched lips, they laid down their lives in the wilderness—their requiem the crackling of the fagots, their funeral anthem the war-whoop of the Indian. Nowhere in the State have there been more stirring scenes than in the pioneer settlements of Lake Superior."

Of course, parched lips and war-whoops were hardly the sort of enticements to turn immigrants' heads, so the author quickly called on the key ingredient in real estate promotion then and now—Bayfield's location, or situation, on the lake.

"If one were to point out on the map of North America a site for a great commercial city, it would be in the immediate vicinity of the 'Apostle Isles.' A city so located would have the command of the mineral trade, the

This pamphlet extolled young Bayfield's many charms, urging pioneers to "emigrate to Bayfield and enjoy the Lake Superior atmosphere."
WHi Image ID 92364

fisheries and the lumber of the entire North. It would become the metropolis of a great commercial empire."

But in suggesting that the next Chicago or St. Louis was there for the making, the author was only getting warmed up. He went on to praise its bay as "one of the safest and most commodious natural harbors in the world," its countryside as hilly "but not generally precipitous," its soil as "good and heavily timbered," and, best of all, "almost entirely free from swamps."

The visitor today who labors up Bayfield's steep hills in summer or white-knuckles up slippery inclines in winter might take issue with part of that description, but even if the sizzle was oversold on some counts, the document generally hit the right notes on the city's assets. Henry Rice, the man who laid out the city site, was described as one of "far-seeing sagacity," and already there were two piers, a large sawmill, a commodious hotel, and buildings "generally larger and more substantial than in most of the new towns on the Lake." Roads were being built, and the contemplated beginning of work on a railroad, which in truth was still decades away, would "create great demand for labor and all kinds of material."

"In short, the location need only be seen to be admired."

Of course, other communities across the developing Midwest were working just as hard to attract immigrants with similarly rosy come-ons. But citing vast expanses

Panorama bird's-eye view of Ashland, Washburn, and Bayfield, on Lake Superior, and the Apostle Islands, ca. 1884.
WHi Image ID 26099

ASHLAND, LAKE SUPERIOR AND THE APOSTLE ISLANDS.

Lake Superior ice-covered shoreline, ca. 1934. Early pamphlets attempting to attract immigrants and other newcomers to the Bayfield area tended to downplay the severity of Lake Superior winters.
WHi Image ID 83680

of public lands available to the would-be farmer willing to leave his family in the East, examine land in Bayfield and make his selections, erect a shanty for shelter, and begin to clear trees from his land, "A poor man can secure a rich farm near Bayfield of 40 or 160 acres, as suits him, for the large sum of $50 or $200!

"Imagine some of these persons on their own farms, the plough in their grasp and their fortune before them."

But do not imagine failure as an option, the guide warned, because the "land near Bayfield will return a greater yield of crops, for less labor," and at prices rivaling those in the East. A fortune could be made in supplying the steamboats and hotels alone with vegetables, the author declared, and what vegetables they would be! A writer in the *Superior Chronicle* had raved about finding onions grown from seed that measured thirteen inches in circumference, tomatoes weighing one pound each, and a parsnip that stretched an impressive thirty-two inches—and that with one end still in the ground.

And here was the part guaranteed to grab certain immigrants' attention: "In fact, we can beat old Ireland in size and quality of potatoes. Let those who reside in cities, and cannot find profitable employment, come here and raise their food out of the bosom of the earth. Thousands have made the experiment, and today are among the wealthiest and most respected of our citizens.

"We assert that a good farmer or mechanic failing to succeed in Bayfield is almost an impossibility. In fact, we would like to hear of one."

Of course, the same northern situation that favored Bayfield with a world-class harbor and ample resources might make for wondrous summers, free of extreme heat and with clean, purifying air that wards off epidemics and endemics. And, citing another writer who had spent time in the area, the guide noted that while the very mention of winter in the far north "conveys almost a sense of misery" to some who watch from afar, "there is nothing relating to Lake Superior more misrepresented, and less understood, than its winters.

"The winter season is said to be, by the oldest residents, the most agreeable part of the year, with plenty of blue sky, fine bracing atmosphere and very little rain from the month of November until April.

"[']Tis true, snow falls to a considerable depth, making the roads level, and filling up all their inequalities and, so far from being an inconvenience, adds greatly to the comfort and happiness of all. This is the season for hilarity and social enjoyment; its lengthened eve is full of fireside joys."

Not mentioned were the long, cold hours spent cutting the firewood to warm that season of hilarity and social enjoyment, though the notion of selling heavy drifting snow as a good thing for filling potholes and leveling ruts might have struck some readers as hilarious on its face. But to immigrants with an eye on the enormous promise of their new homeland, such enticements must have proven irresistible, especially when the guide delivered its knockout summation:

"Settlers, do you want a magnificent climate, lands of unrivalled fertility, no chills, fever, ague, damp and disagreeable weather, sloppy walking, keen, cutting winds, constant political agitation, etc.?

"Then emigrate to Bayfield and enjoy the Lake Superior atmosphere."

Henry M. Rice
Photo courtesy of the
Bayfield Heritage Association,
2001-8-017

Like founder Rice himself, little Bayfield dreamed big. But Rice was also willing to take the small steps necessary to see that Bayfield grew, even if he had to offer rewards. According to the book *Tales of Bayfield Pioneers*, longtime Bayfield newspaper correspondent Eleanor Knight's look at the city's first hundred years, the first white boy born in Bayfield was to a couple named Kitsteiner.

Knight wrote that Rice went to Mr. Kitsteiner with a proposition: "If you will name your son Bayfield, I will give you a town lot."

Mr. Kitsteiner was apparently not a man to look a gift house in the mouth and agreed to name his son Bayfield, thereby earning a choice lot located near the town hall.

Rice wasn't done. When another boy was born in the young city, Knight wrote, Rice said to the child's father, "If you will name the child after me, I will give you ten dollars."

Even if the value of baby naming rights had gone down, the father nonetheless agreed, and Henry M. Rice Hochdanner it was for the city's newest resident.

R. D. PIKE

In 2011 the Bayfield Heritage Association wound up its successful capital campaign by dedicating the new R. D. Pike Research Center, a state-of-the-art facility where those who come to search the city's history will find clues in a room named for a man who made so much history in his day. A dozen of Pike's descendants were present for the dedication, including great-grandson R. Drake Pike, whose $75,000 donation was instrumental in funding the center, so the event neatly tied together Bayfield's past and present. But the name was appropriate beyond financial considerations, because even from his arrival in 1855 as a boy of seventeen, Robinson Derling Pike was involved in almost every significant Bayfield development.

He was present for the founding of the city in March 1856. He served in the Civil War, attaining the rank—and lifetime title—of captain, and later served in the army of the western plains before returning to Bayfield to settle. He would eventually accomplish more than any other early civic leader, though pioneer life was hard and not without

R. D. Pike
Photo courtesy of the Bayfield Heritage Association, 1980-2-03

setbacks. His first shingle mill burned; another he was later involved with at La Pointe exploded, killing three men and injuring others.

But ever the hard-charger, Captain Pike was not dissuaded. He soon undertook a new mill in Bayfield and eventually came to

(continued on next page)

R. D. PIKE

(continued from page 7)
dominate the lumber industry with his famed "Little Daisy" sawmill, which set records for production of the shingles and lumber that he shipped in vast quantities on Lake Superior ships. He led the way in linking Bayfield to the world with telephone service, pushed to get electric lights for city homes and businesses, was instrumental in bringing the state's new fish hatchery to land along Pike's Creek in

1897, toiled tirelessly for better roads, and, as the *Bayfield Press* once noted, "was never so happy as when making improvements."

To accomplish so much, it was said, Pike never strolled through town. Eleanor Knight wrote that he "walked briskly, almost ran, and when he drove he always flipped the reins up and down impatiently, wishing the horses would go faster." His son later recalled riding to town with his father behind Prince, Pike's carriage horse, with the family's fox terrier, Zar, for company. With his father "cussing the horse and cussing the dog all the way to town it was quite a show."

The civic leader impressed his son in other ways, once filling him with pride when Pike introduced the boy to none other than Buffalo Bill, his old friend from the western plains, and later when he "educated" a poor train conductor who had failed to recognize Bayfield's most prominent citizen.

"Young man," he said, "for your edification I am Captain Pike, R. D. Pike, Bayfield Pike, Sawmill Pike, Stone Quarry Pike, Old Man Pike—dammit to hell, don't you know?"

Knight told a similar story of Pike's impatience with a store clerk who was confused about where to ship some goods Pike had ordered. "Send it to Sawmill Pike!

R. D. Pike building, one of the city's locally quarried brownstone structures
WHi Image ID 5775

R. D. PIKE

Pikepole Pike! Captain Pike! R. D. Pike! Pike's Bay Pike! Pike will pay for it." That, she said, became a Bayfield catchphrase that Pike proved true every time he paid for a city improvement, just as his descendants revived the tradition with their contribution to the research center.

R. D. Pike died in March 1906, four days after the fiftieth birthday party of the city he had done so much to improve. His obituary said, "He was always involved with good causes, which had in view the upbuilding of the town and the development of the country." Business was suspended, schools were closed, and flags were lowered in his memory.

The cabins and sawmills that served the city's earliest residents are long gone today, but many historic buildings and homes have

(continued on next page)

The Washington Avenue docks at the turn of the twentieth century. In its commercial heyday Bayfield boasted a bustling waterfront. The Island View Hotel, visible in the upper right quadrant of the photo, was popular with many early tourists.
Photo courtesy of the Bayfield Heritage Association, 2005-194-006

R. D. PIKE

(continued from page 9)
survived—and Bayfield wants to keep it that way. In 1981, on the occasion of the city's 125th birthday, the city established a historic district encompassing nearly sixty downtown blocks over 174 acres. While noting that the city has no identifiable neighborhood of Victorian homes or a town square surrounded by the city's oldest buildings, the city deemed the larger area designation appropriate.

"The visual character of Bayfield, the feel of the place, is as much from the modest homes on the hills as from stately mansions. It is an architectural history and ethic not created solely by prosperity but by periods of just hanging on.

"Bayfield reached the peak of prosperity at the turn of the last century, from about 1880-1910. The fishing, lumbering and brownstone industries were booming, creating wealth from the surrounding wilderness. It was during this period that Bayfield's enduring identity was created. The feel of Bayfield is rooted in the architecture of this boom time, whether it's the sweeping lake view porches of the Queen Anne mansions or the modest steep peaked roofs and clapboard sided houses of the more prevalent class."

As always, the city noted, the past defines the present. "Bayfield's distinct past gives us a glimpse of the Great Lakes, turn of the century fishing village and the city feels an obligation to preserve this view."

THE BAYFIELD FLOOD

Nearly every Wisconsin city with roots in lumbering can tell stories of devastating fires, and more than a few, starting with poor Peshtigo, could fill a book with such tales.

Not many can tell of devastating floods as well, but the 1942 flood that swept through the city of Bayfield was as cataclysmic as any natural disaster lit by lightning or spark. It struck without warning, and before it washed into Lake Superior the rushing rain destroyed downtown buildings and businesses, knocked out telephone and telegraph service, left mountains of dirt and sand on city streets, and even disturbed the sleep of the dead when it opened up the earth at Greenwood Cemetery.

"Dear Dad," resident Mildred LaPointe began in a letter just days later. "If I wrote a whole book I couldn't begin to tell you the terrible thing that has happened to Bayfield."

The event began as just a summer storm—but that is like saying that Paul Bunyan was just a lumberjack. By most accounts just over eight and a half inches of rain fell in twelve hours, a torrential rain that created a river that filled the city's Big Ravine and rushed through the heart of the city. It tossed large boulders about like they were marbles, caused

(continued on next page)

Though many homes and other structures were damaged or destroyed by the flood of 1942, the only loss of life was that of a dog.

Photo by Gil Larsen, courtesy of the Bayfield Heritage Association, 2009-7-14

THE BAYFIELD FLOOD

The 1942 flood ravaged the downtown, including such businesses as Kallerud's Bakery, Sig Anderson's Grocery, and Home Brand Grocery.

Photo by Gil Larsen, courtesy of the Bayfield Heritage Association, 2005-121-3

(continued from page 11)
buildings to collapse, left debris everywhere its waters touched, and left trolling boats beached on bars of sand.

"Bayfield . . . went through a night of disaster last night such as it had never experienced in its history," John B. Chapple wrote in the *Ashland Daily Press*.

Scarcely a business was left untouched. The Theo. Ernst building, constructed of cement blocks, "collapsed completely in one blow without so much as a portion of wall or timber standing," the *Bayfield County Press* wrote. Kallerud Bakery "was completely washed out when a huge boulder diverted

one of the streams toward the back end, pushing out the rear wall and taking all equipment out the front, leaving only the side wall and roof standing." Fire broke out in one building that had already half collapsed, destroying the Johnson Food Shop, L. K. Blanchard's law office, Mrs. O'Connell's beauty parlor, and the personal belongings of the residents of the apartments that had been upstairs.

The offices of the *Bayfield County Press* were heavily damaged, publisher William G. Reque reported, with press, stereotype, and mailing equipment "buried in five feet of sand topped by a goodly supply of rain water, well

THE BAYFIELD FLOOD

stirred, and caked to a beautiful chocolate brown." But "in spite of 'hell and high water'" the paper was published in somewhat abbreviated form and only a few days late with a banner headline that read "$750,000 Flood Damage Devastates City."

Beyond the physical loss there was the emotional pain of many families whose loved ones had been washed out of the ground at Greenwood Cemetery. The cemetery, high on the hill above the city, had been a gift from early Bayfield resident Isaac Wing. The raging waters washed out about thirty graves, opening caskets and leaving bodies, and sometimes body parts, strewn around the grounds. Recovering the disgorged bodies and returning them to their graves was the job of a crew of undertakers led by Harvey Gildersleeve of Bayfield and the fire chief, Ed Erickson. Several local women stood guard on the road to the cemetery to keep gawkers and reporters at bay while the grisly work was done. In the end, bodies that could not be identified were placed in a single grave, identified in the morticians' final report not by name but by such descriptions as "remains of a very short man, bald head, white fringe of hair on edges . . ."

In 2007, when workers on a downtown street construction project came across human bones, it was yet another echo of the flood's lasting effect on the city. As Mildred LaPointe had sadly concluded her letter to her father, "Our pretty little town will never be the same again, Dad."

THE APOSTLE ISLANDS AND Lake Superior.

2 Train's Arrival Puts Bayfield on Track

T he visitor to modern-day Bayfield will find many wondrous sights, from carefully preserved architecture in the downtown historic district to orchards rich with apples and berries, from sleek sailboats in busy marinas to quiet kayaks slipping onto the lake, and even the curious local specialty known as whitefish livers.

What the visitor will not find is the once-imagined port city to rival Chicago in importance, or even Superior. The Bayfield Land Company, created with such big dreams, fell victim to the financial panic of 1857, which caused a sharp slowdown in growth for most new communities in the far North. Despite all of the town's boosters who claimed its "situation" unmatched, the fact was that Bayfield was a rather isolated place, reachable only by water in its early years and then only when the water was free of icy impediments. While travel over ice and snow on foot and by dogsled was common in early years, it took until 1871 to connect Bayfield with Superior by way of a rough and uncomfortable wagon road, but the route did serve its purpose as a window to the larger world.

Settlers settled and Bayfield grew, and occasionally shrunk when its struggling citizens moved on. The 1860 census showed a population of 353 but with 38 unoccupied dwellings, haunting reminders of the difficulty of making new homes in a place one newspaper later described as "howling wilderness," a description most certainly not part of that early appeal to settlers.

The Homestead Act of 1862 lured more settlers to the Chequamegon region, though farming in the far North was a daunting challenge. Additional residents arrived after the Civil War, seeking opportunities in logging, fishing, and other work.

It was likely the very isolation that made life so difficult also made the city truly become a community. William Knight, a native of Delaware who would become one of early Bayfield's leading figures, arrived in 1869 at age twenty-six and later noted in his

The train depot in Bayfield. According to Marilyn Van Sant of the Bayfield Heritage Association, the Bayfield passenger depot was approximately where the intersection of Manypenny and Broad Streets is now, across from the current Chamber of Commerce office. It was not named Manypenny at the time but was known as Fant Avenue. The roundhouse was a block farther down the street.

Photo by Gil Larsen, courtesy of the Bayfield Heritage Association, 1980-2-390

cheer after cheer. This was a big day of impromptu celebrations, and it was followed by a big night of celebrations.

"At last Bayfield had a train."

It is from Eleanor Knight, who collected many of her historical accounts for the city's centennial celebration in 1956, that we get a picture of daily life in early Bayfield and the Chequamegon region. There was hardship, yes, but humorous days as well. There was often sadness but also celebration.

Bayfield was known by two early nicknames, the Harbor City and the Fountain City. The former is easily understood; the latter came from the many fountains outside of Bayfield homes, often stocked with trout that tourists enjoyed watching and even feeding. Visitors arriving from the south today still pass Fountain Garden Park at the edge of the city, and a lovely and welcoming vestige of old Bayfield it is.

Then, as now, the Fourth of July was cause for great celebration marked by flag waving, boat rides, picnics, baseball, firecrackers, and fireworks. The first US flag to fly over Bayfield was a handmade version raised by businessman Andrew Tate on July 4, 1858. (Replicas of the same flag can be seen flying on some Bayfield flagpoles today. In 2010 the Bayfield Heritage Association produced replicas of the city's "Grand Old Flag" as a means of raising funds to restore Tate's original banner, now part of the BHA collection.) The same brass cannon that greeted the arrival of the Omaha line, which

The first US flag to fly over Bayfield was a handmade version raised by businessman Andrew Tate on July 4, 1858. Replicas of the original flag can now be viewed flying in front of city homes and businesses.
Photo courtesy of the Bayfield Heritage Association, BHA-DSC_4179

had been left behind in Bayfield by soldiers who came during an earlier Sioux Indian scare, was a traditional part of Fourth of July celebrations and, in fact, most other special occasions in the city.

The cannon, Knight noted, "took an active part in Bayfield's history. It developed the quality of Mary's little lamb, for everywhere that Bayfielders went, the cannon was sure to go.

"It became traditional for the cannon to boom at sunrise on the Glorious Fourth. Its thundering tones were used to spread the tidings of political victories and defeats.

"Whenever there was deep emotion in Bayfield, our cannon gave voice to it."

There were other traditions, less noisy but a bit more of a nuisance. Long before the advent of today's free-range cattle, Knight wrote often of cows that roamed Bayfield streets at will. If a fence was built, it was as much to keep cows away as people because "cows were the number one problem in Bayfield for years. Every place in Bayfield had cow fences, because the cows ran at large and the people take cover. That's the way it was."

Three men and a flag: The man on the right is Andrew Tate, who came up with Bayfield's first flag that is on the wall behind them. On the left is John Hanley. The man in the middle is unidentified.
Photo courtesy of the Bayfield Heritage Association, 2001-8-063

View of Bayfield, ca. 1892, painted by Alice Downs, a Bayfield resident
WHi Image ID 93629

Woe to those who failed to take cover, because with their clanging bells the cows disturbed the peace, frightened pedestrians, and occasionally posed real danger. One little boy had his collarbone broken by a cow that declined to yield way, and women in long dresses tired of trying to step over cows that took their rest on the downtown's wooden sidewalks. Sometimes cows forced passersby into stores for cover, though if being forced to find refuge bothered the pedestrians it likely pleased the merchants. Even such a leading citizen as William Knight was moved to drastic action by one canny bovine that learned how to unhook the cow gate in front of his house, permitting her and trailing cows to enter his garden and cause damage at will.

"Knight warned the owner, but it did no good," Eleanor Knight wrote later. "Finally the end of his patience was reached. The bell clanged under his window just once too often. He got out of his bed, loaded his twenty-two, raised the window and fired."

It was a bull's-eye, so to speak.

"The cowbell pealed wildly, circled the house and diminished in the dark distance. It was not until the next morning that the course of her flight was traced. She had rushed out of the yard, down the front steps and across the street to the Presbyterian Church yard where she dropped dead.

"Mr. Knight paid the owner $35. That was a fair price for a cow in those days."

Such hazards aside, the little city did manage to grow in its first decades, if not to the lofty size and stature of those early rosy claims. By 1885, a census showed Bayfield with a population of 1,409, with three churches, two schools, a lumber mill, four fish dealers, numerous supporting businesses, a roller rink, and even its own brass band. Still, by then it was a more realistic local newspaper that concluded, "It is not expected that a great city will spring up here in a season, but it is confidently expected that here will always be found a live, prosperous, growing town and the most desirable place for a residence on the shores of the 'Great Unsalted Sea.'"

On that note, the *Bayfield County Press* got it half right. Bayfield was not always prosperous or growing, but a desirable residence it was, and still is.

Bayfield panorama, 1910. Note the deforestation in the surrounding hills, the result of heavy lumbering in the area.
Courtesy of Bayfield Heritage Association, 1981-8-1-006 thru 001

had bought R. D. Pike's operation after Pike's death in 1906, similarly operated multiple camps on the Apostle Islands.

Lumbering continued even as the era's eventual death became undeniable. Some sawmills burned and were not rebuilt because it was clear the future would bring changes, and others were closed one by one as supply fell. In 1919 there were still three hundred men employed in the Wachsmuth mill and lumberyard, but just five years later the crew consisted of but ninety workers. In *People and Places: A Human History of the Apostle Islands*, Jane C. Busch noted that the *Bayfield County Press* was not alarmed at the mill's closing because other industries were developing.

Lumber camp steam hauler near Squaw Bay on the Bayfield Peninsula
Photo courtesy of the National Park Service

However, the local paper certainly recognized that in the decline of lumbering an important chapter of local history was closing, noting with sadness, "The smoke (of the logging train) will no longer be seen rising in vast clouds, the whistle will no longer resound along the lake and through the hills; the thunder of the logs as they plunge into the bay and the sounds of the woodsman's axe and saw as he fells the lofty pine and cedar may be spoken of in verse and story, but will be known only in memory."

One of those nostalgic moments came on September 9, 1924, when some fifty Bayfielders gathered to watch the last hemlock log go through the Wachsmuth mill, and to listen for nine long minutes while the shrill mill whistle signaled the official end of the era.

The Lullabye Lumber Company logged on Outer Island from the 1930s through the 1950s, one of the last commercial lumbering operations in the Apostle Islands. This 1956 photo shows chainsaw operator Lyle Yancy preparing to cut a large yellow birch.
Photo courtesy of the National Park Service

Lullaby logging crane on Outer Island, 1950s
Photo from the Don Jaskowiak collection, courtesy of the National Park Service

There would be small-scale commercial lumbering after that, however. In 1936 the Lullabye Furniture Company of Stevens Point purchased all of Outer Island, with about eight thousand acres of standing timber, to get wood for its line of children's furniture and toys. It did not begin taking wood off Oak Island until 1942 (eventually using a surplus World War II landing craft, the *Outer Island*, that is still in use in Bayfield today), and later Lullabye began getting timber from Outer Island as well.

By the 1950s, Lullabye was one of the largest builders of children's furniture in the United States. It is entirely possible that many of today's visitors spent time in cradles created from trees from the Apostle Islands years before they came to see the islands as tourists.

And it is just as likely that many visitors would be shocked to see photographs of the islands after they were logged over as much as a century ago. It took decades to grow new forests, but in time the new growth did come. Though today's island forests may not be as majestic as the virgin stands that existed at one time, they at least make the Apostles a beautiful refuge again. Time can't heal all wounds, but eventually it can cover up those caused by the woodsman's axe and saw.

The *Outer Island*, shown here when nearly lost in a wintry accident, was once a World War II landing craft. In 2004 the PBS series *History Detectives* determined that, contrary to local legend, the vessel was not used in the Normandy invasion in June 1944, but it did see action in August 1944 during the Operation Dragoon invasion of southern France, the second-largest landing of World War II. The *Outer Island* is still used as a workboat around Bayfield today.

The National Park Service maintains hiking trails on several of the Apostle Islands, including Oak Island.

Photo courtesy of the National Park Service

4 A Business in Building Blocks

As the opening of Chicago's 1893 World's Columbian Exposition neared, entrepreneurs and assorted swells across the nation and around the globe prepared grand-scale exhibits aimed at leaving fairgoers in awe of their power and invention. This was the fair that would give the world the Ferris wheel, the first electric exhibits, and the famed White City that revolutionized architecture of the time—and later incited a devilish work of literature (*The Devil in the White City* by Erik Larson)—so no dream was too big.

Except one, perhaps. It came from the Chequamegon Bay region, where the preeminent quarry owner, Frederick Prentice, was inspired to produce a giant brownstone monument in the shape of an obelisk that would not only inform the world about his stone-rich quarry but also amaze the public by how it towered over the fair, taller even than the legendary Egyptian obelisk known as Cleopatra's Needle in New York City.

No small dreamer, our man Prentice. At his quarry at Houghton Point near Washburn, Prentice's workers in 1892 indeed fashioned an obelisk that measured 10 feet square at the base and 4 feet square at the top, and stretched a wondrous 115 feet in height, carrying enough mass to weigh in at a tidy four hundred tons. But like the man who builds an airplane in his garage that ends up wider than the door it must pass through, Prentice had dreamed too big. The obelisk proved too heavy to be shipped on any lake vessel or railcar available, and a specially designed scow was deemed too expensive. In the end, Prentice sent four smaller monoliths off to Chicago, including statues of an Indian chief and a Wisconsin badger. At least a bit of brownstone made the fair, though whether the brownstone badger impressed the world was not mentioned by historians.

It would be easy to lump the brownstone-quarrying era with all of the other boom-and-bust events in the region's past but for one significant difference. While beaver

Workers at an unidentified Chequamegon Bay sandstone quarry. By the 1880s at least ten commercial quarries were developed in the Chequamegon Bay region—on the mainland as well as on various islands.

Photo courtesy of the National Park Service

and Juliet balconies and an attached observation tower, along with carved brownstone fireplaces and chimneys, and for its cedar shingles the elaborate residence on a rather isolated little island became known as Cedar Bark Lodge.

Alas, love is unpredictable. By many accounts, Prentice's young bride was so underwhelmed by the dwelling that she never went back after her first view of the cottage, which was used only sporadically before it was torn down in the 1930s.

Cedar Bark Lodge on Hermit Island, Apostle Islands, ca. 1910. Cedar Bark Lodge was also known as the Hermitage. Built on Hermit Island in the early 1890s for Frederick Prentice and his new bride, the house was never occupied by Frederick and Mrs. Prentice.
WHi Image ID 3192

By ca. 1926, when this photo was taken, Cedar Bark Lodge had fallen into disrepair.
WHi Image ID 4385

Evidence of the quarrying industry can still be found on the Apostle Islands, including on Basswood Island, shown here.

Photo by Tamara Thomsen, Wisconsin Historical Society

The Panic of 1893 was one reason for a drop in demand for Lake Superior brownstone, but by then alternative construction methods using steel and brick and changing design styles had taken a toll as well. By the early 1900s, only small-scale harvesting of brownstone was taking place, and soon even that would be just a memory.

But in the peak years of quarrying, brownstone from the Chequamegon region was shipped throughout the Midwest to build beautiful libraries and courthouses, churches and residences in such cities as Minneapolis and St. Paul, Chicago, Toledo, Cleveland, Detroit, and beyond, and some went as far as New York City. Today, visitors to the region can search out quarry walls on Basswood Island, Stockton Island, and along Highway 13 south of Bayfield, where the scars left by quarrymen attest to a once-vibrant industry.

But better evidence remains in the still-impressive brownstone buildings of Bayfield, Washburn, and Ashland. Oddly, more structures were built of brownstone from the Bayfield area in some faraway cities than closer to home, but enough were constructed locally to leave the region with a signature look. In Bayfield, brownstone structures include the former Bayfield County Courthouse, now the headquarters of the Apostle Island National Lakeshore; several downtown commercial buildings; the Bayfield City Hall; and Holy Family Catholic Church. In Washburn, the public library was built of brownstone, as was the bank that now houses the Washburn Cultural Center and historical museum.

If he could come back today, Frederick Prentice might take special note of that last one. In front of the museum entrance is a twenty-seven-foot brownstone obelisk, a pint-sized tribute to Prentice's monumental dream.

This photo shows the remains of a quarry pier off Basswood Island. It is a wooden crib filled with stone that at one time supported a dock above. Ships would have pulled up to this pier to load brownstone from the island, as pictured in the photo on page 37.

Photo by Tamara Thomsen, Wisconsin Historical Society

Built in 1890 by A.C. Probert, Washburn's "Old Bank Building" is listed in both the State and National Register of Historic Places. The building is now home to the Washburn Area Historical Society Museum and the Washburn Cultural Center. The obelisk is a smaller-scale version of a much larger one intended for, but never delivered to, the Chicago World's Fair.

Photo by Barbara Walsh, Wisconsin Historical Society

5 Treasured Islands, and Island Treasure?

A first-time visitor's impression of today's Apostle Islands could easily be misleading, but the misperception would be perfectly understandable. Viewed from the highway that runs along Wisconsin's northern edge, from a kayak bobbing on Chequamegon Bay, or from the top deck of a tour boat on one of its daily circuits, a visitor might conclude that these islands of sylvan green set against the deep blue of Lake Superior have been largely unaffected by the hand of man, that these forested oases in the water are the last wild places in a state that was long ago tamed in every way.

It is true that today the islands are managed as wilderness, but that is hardly to say they are wilderness in its purest definition of a natural environment that has not been changed by human activity. Rich in natural resources, the islands have over the past few hundred years been hunted and fished, logged and farmed, berried and quarried. On some of the islands there have been homes and roads, fish camps and logging shacks, roads and short stretches of railroad, and even a school on Sand Island for a time. Look closely at the islands and the evidence is there in the crumbled foundations that survive where buildings stood, in the remnant orchards that tell of human touch, in the stone-strong bones of a onetime quarry, or in ruts that were once a road.

Today the islands may resemble the wild places that greeted the early Native Americans who made their homes among the islands, or the first white missionaries and explorers, and if they do it is credit to the power of preservation championed by, perhaps foremost among many others, former Wisconsin senator Gaylord Nelson, who wrote in the introduction to Harold Jordahl's book on the establishment of the Apostle Islands National Lakeshore that "this is a unique collection of islands. There is not another collection of islands of this significance in the continental boundaries of the United States."

The Apostle Islands
viewed from above
© John & Ann Mahan

And many who live and play in this special place most heartily agree.

The beautiful archipelago known as the Apostle Islands is made up of twenty-two islands—though there were more in the relatively recent past—which raises the obvious question of why these polka-dot parcels of land in the waters off the tip of the Bayfield peninsula were named for a biblical dozen. The likely answer is that the French who prepared the first maps of the new world favored giving religious names to new places, and in a day when there are fully fourteen schools in the Big Ten conference, who are we to feel superior about early French math?

If their collective moniker is not issue enough, the islands' individual names can be puzzling as well. A number of the islands have worn different names through the years. Henry Rowe Schoolcraft, an early visitor to the region and later an important Indian agent, attempted to change the name from the Apostle Islands to the Federation Islands, each of which would be named for a state of the union. Madeline Island would have become Virginia if Schoolcraft had prevailed, but although Michigan Island does wear the name of one state of the union, that proposal otherwise went nowhere. Still, while the names attached to islands appear to be permanent, a few local residents with sufficient mileage can sometimes be heard using earlier names when describing the islands. According to Duncanson's *Guide to the Apostle Islands*, South Twin Island's original Indian name meant Rabbit Island, Rocky Island's original name meant Maple Sugar Island, and Manitou's Indian name meant spirit, or god.

Without question the most colorful naming story is attached to Hermit Island and the "Hermit Wilson" who inspired it. It is such a good yarn that, however sketchy the actual details, it deserves to be told here. As longtime park ranger, writer, and retired historian for the Apostle Islands National Lakeshore Bob Mackreth put it in one of his many fine stories of island life, "The tale of the Hermit is a story filled with violence, romance, and wealth. Or maybe not—it's hard to say. You see, since there was nothing written about the Hermit during his lifetime, writers and tale spinners over the ensuing century and a half have felt free to make things up as they went along."

Even his supposed name, William Wilson, is subject to some doubt, as were the circumstances of his early life, though various tellings will suggest there was a woman somewhere at the heart of his dark spirit. At any rate, Wilson eventually made his way to Madeline Island in 1841, where he became a barrel maker for the legendary island

Family gathering on Basswood Island, 1916. Those picnicking include Harriet Webb, C. A. Hull, H. W. Rodgers, Mrs. J. Austin, Elizabeth Baker, Mrs. J. L. Abernathy, and two Austin children.
WHi Image ID 1973

An abandoned house on Hermit Island. This photo was taken in 1930 for the Kelsey Report, the National Park Service's first survey of the Apostle Islands. Could this have been the home of hermit of legend Willie Wilson?

Photo courtesy of the National Park Service

ruler "King" John Bell. Sadly for Wilson, but happily for his own legend, when the two strong-willed men came to blows a few years later, Bell had the stronger hand, knocking Wilson to the ground with a single great blow.

Wilson, humiliated, declared "he would never stay on an island where he was not the best man, and so loaded a canoe with provisions and set off to an island where no man would be his better," Mackreth wrote.

He made that happen by living alone in a hermit-like existence. He continued to make barrels but resisted visitors, and his trips to the mainland for goods were rare and brief. Still, he drew attention; some said he paid for goods with fancy Mexican coins, and rumors spread that Wilson had a treasure in gold or silver squirreled away on his island. When he died—whiskey is often claimed as the cause—the rumors of hidden gold intensified, and the man who had wished simply to be left alone left a mystery for the ages.

No one, in case you are wondering, has ever found it.

The simple geologic explanation of how the islands came to be is that water and ice in the form of glaciers over millions of years conspired to shape their sandstone cliffs and sandy shorelines. Waves and weather over many centuries have left their own changes and continue to reshape the islands in subtle ways yet today. Some of the most dramatic formations are the sea caves on the north shore of Devil's Island, at Swallow Point on Sand Island, and on the mainland off Meyers Beach Road at the western end of the National Lakeshore.

Devil's Island on Lake Superior, outermost of the Apostle Islands group, is honeycombed with sea caves, making it a favorite destination for kayakers.
Photo courtesy of the National Park Service

Science, of course, is reliable, if sometimes dry. If you would prefer a more colorful way to explain the Apostle Islands, consider the creation story of the Ojibwe people who made their homes here long before the first French traders and voyageurs arrived. The legend involves Winnebozho, the first man, who was in dispute with a Water Spirit who, in an attempt to drown his adversary, caused the waters to rise until they covered the entire Earth. However, Winnebozho was gifted with supernatural powers and escaped drowning by climbing a tall pine tree and commanding it to rise above the water. When the spirit, seeing he had been bested, allowed waters to recede, Winnebozho climbed down and was met by an otter, which he directed to swim down to the bottom and bring up some earth so he could create land. The otter failed, as did a mink Winnebozho similarly charged. Then he sent a muskrat on the same task, but after the muskrat struggled to reach bottom he reappeared on the surface, drowned.

Winnebozho picked up the muskrat and found grains of sand in its claws, and after breathing new life into the animal he began to blow the grains of sand long distances over the water. Every grain, by this legend, grew into an island.

The Michigan Island Lighthouse was the first lighthouse in the Apostle Islands. It began operation in 1857.
WHi Image ID 47235

Like children in large families, the islands share obvious attributes, yet each possesses its own distinct identity. The early Bayfield newspaperman Samuel S. Fifield once wrote, "Almost every island has its own peculiarities, its bit of romance or its own curiosity to exhibit. Sailing among them they bear a considerable likeness to each other, but close inspection dissolves the illusion for they differ very materially."

They range in size from tiny Gull Island, which peeks just ten feet above the surface of the water and covers just three acres, to Madeline, which boasts twenty-four square miles of land surface. The only developed island, Madeline is the year-round home to several hundred hardy residents and as many as twenty-five hundred to three thousand summer residents, and it is the only island not part of the Apostle Island National Lakeshore.

The islands today are a playground for sightseers, hikers, paddlers, power and sail boaters, birders, and other outdoor enthusiasts. So long as care is taken to protect it, the stunning beauty of the Chequamegon region is one resource that does not play out, as the timber stocks and fish populations did in the past. But the often-unruly lake that surrounds the islands can be a hostile environment, and in the early days when commercial shipping was becoming a force on the big lake, the government enlisted some of the islands to serve the cause of commerce.

GEOLOGY

Historian Bob Mackreth says it is important for visitors to understand that while they are in a place described as wilderness, they are certainly not the first to set foot in it.

"Wherever you pitch your tent or beach your kayak in the Apostle Islands, someone's been there before. If you think it's a good place to land, you're not the first; a geologist named Bela Hubbard already knew that in 1840," he wrote, quoting Hubbard as having said, "As it is an object to select a good halting place, and particularly a convenient camping ground, we very frequently select spots which have been the camping grounds of the voyageurs and of the Indians almost from time immemorial."

Today it can be said that geologists have long left their own footprints on these intriguing islands. While most of us look at the red sandstone cliffs on Lake Superior, at the caves carved by wind and water, and at the ever-changing islands and think only in terms of stunning scenery, geologists

Interactions of land and water create ever-changing formations in the sandstone cliffs of the Apostle Islands.
Photo by Tamara Thomsen, Wisconsin Historical Society

GEOLOGY

see a fascinating laboratory in which to revel in their special science. As Hamilton Nelson Ross put it in his history of the area, "Probably the Lake Superior region is the oldest of the known world, the first to emerge from a global ocean. Because of its geological age, its subjection to some of nature's most violent treatment and to subsequent erosion, part of the earth's most profound secrets have been exposed here to human eyes."

In *A Guidebook to the Geology of Lake Superior's Apostle Islands National Lakeshore*, Edward B. Nuhfer and Mary P. Dalles note that there are three geologic aspects to consider, beginning with the sandstone bedrock that dates back more than one billion years. Much later, some ten thousand to twelve thousand years ago, the region was greatly affected by glaciers that cut the high bluffs and became the main source for the beaches and sandspits enjoyed today. Finally there is the "geology of the present," the interactions of water and land that produce such changes as collapsing rock arches or crumbling banks as a result of ongoing wave action or powerful storms.

"The degree to which all three aspects may be observed within the islands makes the area a virtual treasure for the outdoorsman, the naturalist and certainly the student of geology," they wrote.

There are three distinct formations of sandstone that make up the islands' base rock, the Chequamegon, Orienta, and Devils Island formations that were deposited by streams hundreds of millions of years ago. The upper- and lower-most layers (the Chequamegon and Orienta formations) are in the Precambrian Bayfield Group and were deposited by northeastward-flowing braided streams (streams that flow in several channels that divide and reunite). The Devils Island formation (which is not exclusive to that island), between the sandstones, represents deposition across sand flats that were intermittently covered by shallow ponded water. Later, Pleistocene ice advances repeatedly reshaped the Apostles region, the most recent about twelve thousand years ago. In the wake of those glaciers, "melt waters varied drastically in elevation and longevity," according to the National Park Service, and what was known as Glacial Lake Duluth submerged most of the Bayfield peninsula and the islands. As new drainages opened up and lake levels fell, the Apostles became part of the peninsula, but later during extreme rises in lake levels the Apostles were separated from the mainland to form the archipelago.

Most visible to even amateur geologists is the work of centuries of wave action,

(continued on next page)

RACE WEEK

(continued from page 57)
racer Jim Vaudreuil, in something of an understatement, "Bayfield became a pretty good sailing destination."

The regatta opens with a race around the Apostle Islands, a sixty-six-nautical-mile challenge that serves as a sort of work-out-the-kinks warm-up for captains and crews. "It's a great test," Vaudreuil said. "A lot of boats from all over come for that, and then they get a day off and then start with Race Week."

One thing that has changed over the years is that boats have gotten faster, said Bill Peterson, whose fifty-foot sailboat *Chewbacca*, a winner of many Midwestern events, is a perfect example. But Peterson, who has competed in more than twenty-five Race Weeks, said many sailors from such Lake Superior ports as Thunder Bay, Duluth, and Houghton return each year because of the event's tradition and constancy. "Our basic program hasn't changed much, and when we ask what we should change they say, 'Don't change it.'"

Still, the effort to get more casual sailors involved is important for the future of racing on Chequamegon Bay, Vaudreuil said. "It's really kind of an exciting thing, because there's a thousand boats up there. How do we get them to turn out? We're focusing on growing that. That's our vision with this mid-distance, formerly cruising class [event], trying to get these people excited and interested."

For serious racers, though, having a full week set aside for racing sets the Bayfield regatta apart from many other events. As the magazine *Sailing World* noted in 2011, "You know Bayfield Race Week is old school because it's a race week that actually takes place over the course of a week. Too many of these events have been neutered down to a long weekend, or even just a weekend.

"That sort of nose-to-the-grindstone thinking hasn't penetrated this tiny Lake Superior hamlet. The Monday-through-Friday race week can't be beat. The weekend before allows travel and/or practice. The weekend after, time to shake off the hangover and the boat bites so the regulars can show up for work on Monday at least partially refreshed . . . what better way to tour the Apostle Islands National Lakeshore?"

Or to win, as they say on television, fabulous prizes, or nearly so.

"At the end of the day," Vaudreuil said, it's all about bragging rights. "Win and they hand you a thousand-dollar coffee mug."

6 Making a Living from the Lake

The sight is as familiar in Bayfield as apple blossoms in the orchards or ice cream in the hand of a tourist staring at real estate ads in a downtown window. Out on the lake, often late in the day, a low-slung fishing tug labors back into harbor, a stodgy workhorse of a craft compared to the show-pony sail and power boats that dominate the big blue water, trailed by a cloud of noisy gulls begging for scraps of a hard day's catch.

Hours later that catch will turn into another familiar Bayfield sight—a dinner of fresh lake trout or whitefish, perhaps grilled or cedar planked, sautéed or fried. Start with an appetizer of whitefish livers served with peppers and onions and your Bayfield experience will be complete, and oh so historically correct.

Though commercial fishing is no longer the booming industry it was in years past, working fishing boats are still a common sight on Apostle Islands waters today.
Photo by Tamara Thomsen, Wisconsin Historical Society

Hauling in whitefish off
Bear Island
Photo by Gil Larsen,
courtesy of the Bayfield
Heritage Association,
1980-2-211

High school teams in the far north come by their names honestly. The Ashland Oredockers take their name from the long piers that stretched into Lake Superior to ship ore from the iron mines to mills throughout the Great Lakes. The Mellen Granite Diggers are so called because of longtime granite quarries in the area, and the Washburn Castle Guards were inspired by the city's turreted first high school that everyone thought resembled a castle. We'll leave the Hurley Midgets—and that school's girls' teams, the Midgettes—for another discussion, but to any list of aptly named school teams you would have to include the Bayfield Trollers, teams that honor a small city's longtime fishing tradition.

Logging and quarrying were important parts of the local economy during their respective boom times, but it was commercial fishing, harvesting the rich resources of Lake Superior for more than a century, that came to identify Bayfield both in Wisconsin and across the land. Though fishermen still ply the waters of Chequamegon Bay and beyond, commercial fishing was as much a story of boom and bust as logging and quarrying. But in the way that fishing dominated the economy for decades and touched almost every part of the community, especially during the hectic herring run, fishing became a major component of the city's DNA. Not without reason did the *Bayfield County Press* declare proudly in 1905, "The fishing industry has given a name and fame to Bayfield all over the United States."

That distinction stands to reason, of course, given the city's location on the shore of fish-rich Lake Superior. Even so, for many years the little city on Wisconsin's northernmost peninsula was the biggest fishing community on the entire lake. U-rah-rah, Trollers.

Of course, fish was a valued resource for the Ojibwe (and other, much earlier Native inhabitants of the area) and for the early French traders, missionaries, and other explorers long before commercial fishing began. Species including trout, whitefish, sturgeon, pike, and herring were caught by hook and line, spear, or nets and eaten fresh or smoked. The fur traders bartered with Indian fishermen. As early as the 1830s, the American Fur Company established the first commercial venture in the Chequamegon region when it began shipping barrels of salted fish from La Pointe and other stations on Lake Superior to Detroit and other markets, employing coopers as well as fishermen. The company's fishing endeavor was disrupted by a financial panic in 1837, and for the most part commercial efforts dwindled for several decades.

That changed in 1870 when the N & F Boutin fishing operation moved from Two Rivers, on Wisconsin's Lake Michigan shoreline, to Bayfield, bringing with them more than a hundred fishermen and their families, 650 gill nets, the schooner *Alice Craig*, and other boats. By December of that year the number of fishermen was said to exceed two hundred men and the industry was firmly, and permanently, established.

As Eleanor Knight put it in her centennial history of Bayfield pioneers, "In 1871 navigation opened on April 11, the ice cleared on Ashland Bay on April 12, the light-houses went on April 13 and the schooner *Alice Craig* departed for Ashland Bay with fish nets and crew. From that day to the present some member of the Boutin family has been in the fish business at Bayfield."

Catch of lake trout displayed by three fishermen on the pier at Little Sand Bay, about 1955. From left to right are Martin Johnson, Hermy Johnson, and Myron Lohma.
WHi Image ID 49874

By 1885 Bayfield was determined by the US Commission of Fish and Fisheries to be the leading fishing community on Lake Superior. A study showed 182 fishermen made Bayfield their home port, and others were employed in barrel making, packing, and shipping fish to markets. Whitefish was the most important species, and Bayfield fishermen were most adept at catching them; in 1885 the fishermen from Bayfield and Ashland were responsible for nearly half of the whitefish caught in all of Lake Superior.

Perhaps it was inevitable that such pressure on white-fish populations would cause a decline in fish numbers. When that did occur fishermen turned more attention to lake trout and, by the 1890s, to herring, smaller fish that had found prime habitat in Apostle Island waters. The recent arrival of railroad service to Bayfield made ship-ping fish easier, and the industry continued to drive the local economy. While the Boutins remained one of the largest operations, another major player arrived when the

Memohead from the A. Booth Packing Company of Bayfield, Wisconsin, 1895

WHi Image ID 8902

A. Booth Packing Company developed packinghouses, net sheds, icehouses, and other facilities on the city's lakefront. Booth was such a dominant player in the business, and some fishermen were so tied to the company's might, that some called the company "Papa Booth." But other dealers worked the Bayfield harbor as well, and any visitor arriving by boat would know instantly, by sight if not by olfactory evidence, that Bayfield was a fishing town.

While the initial wave of fishermen were mostly French Canadians, along with a large number of Ojibwe fishermen, in the 1890s numerous Scandinavians began arriving and soon became the dominant ethnic group in the Chequamegon region. In her *People and Places: A Human History of the Apostle Islands*, Jane C. Busch says that most of the first Norwegians who moved to Bayfield came from coastal towns in Norway and were attracted to a place that felt familiar but offered a less difficult living and working environment.

"The old story was these Norwegians got into New York Harbor from Norway," a former Bayfield fisherman, Jack Erickson, once said. "They'd give 'em a bowl of snuff and staple a 'Booth Fisheries' tag on their back, put 'em on a train, and send them to Bayfield."

However they got there, many felt they had found a place just like home, only better. A sign over a doorway at one fish camp on Rocky Island read, "Ya vi hard et godt en Amerika. And it could be better," Busch wrote. The Norwegian translated to "Yes, we have it good in America."

The business was handed down from generation to generation, just as boats and nets were passed down. Jack Erickson, in an oral history recorded long after his retirement from fishing, recalled joining his grandfather and father on the lake at an age when boys elsewhere were playing baseball or reading comic books.

"I was a kid on a boat with my dad [during] high school, grade school," Erickson said. "Just along for the ride, even before they put a pair of oilers on you."

Fishing offered the independence of self-employment and an office as big as the great lake itself, but it was not an easy life. Most fishermen would live from spring to fall at fish camps throughout the Apostle Islands, and dealers would send boats out to collect fish and deliver supplies. Some fishermen established homes on the islands but many others stayed in rustic dwellings, making only occasional trips to the mainland. Weather could be notoriously fickle, and boating accidents were only too familiar. Though annual catches would rise and fall for various reasons, overall the industry prospered well into the 1900s; in 1920 the US Department of Commerce counted 345 fishermen in Bayfield County (Cornucopia, Herbster, and Port Wing were all active fishing communities as well), and as late as 1947 there were an estimated seventy-five to one hundred fishing boats working area waters.

Eventually a small community of fishermen and families was established on Sand Island, more than 90 percent of them Norwegian or Norwegian American. The community had a small school, post office, cooperative store and other businesses, including, for a brief period, telephone service to Bayfield by way of an underwater cable that linked island and mainland. It was soon severed, though, and proved too costly to repair.

Perhaps like many other jobs, there was a routine to commercial fishing that approached what some looking back today would describe as monotonous. In winter, when fishing was not active, most days were spent mending nets; in season, lifting nets to retrieve each day's catch was the fisherman's equivalent of a farmer milking cows. It simply had to be done, and there were few off days unless Mother Nature stepped in with nasty weather.

Building, boats, and fish net drying racks on South Twin Island, ca. 1915
WHi Image ID 47206

7 The Beguiling Madeline

Over to Old La Pointe, rowing to Old La Pointe
Summer is here, we'll have our share, ferry carry us over there
We miss the boat back, we don't care!
We'll dance with the ghosts of old New France
On the Island . . . on the Rock . . . on the shores of Old La Pointe.
—©Warren Nelson; used with permission

As popular as Madeline Island has long been with summer residents and short-term vacationers, it might be even more popular with big-city newspaper writers who come to extol its beauty, to marvel at the hardiness of islanders who make it home year-round, and generally to enjoy a "work" trip that ends daily in glorious Technicolor sunsets.

But there is a challenge to such labor. As one visiting writer put it many years ago, "So much has been said about Madeline Island in Lake Superior that I'm stumped for a new descriptive word . . . I'll just call it 'idyllic' and stick to it."

It works, and long has worked. As John O. Holzhueter noted in the beginning of his book *Madeline Island and the Chequamegon Region*, the first visitor of record who arrived in 1659 pronounced it "beautiful," and another nineteenth-century first-time observer went into wordsmith overdrive to report, "It looks like a fairy scene, and everything about it is enchantment."

Island residents might quarrel with that when property tax bills arrive or when inhospitable winter holds the island in its grip. An island in winter is by definition an isolated place. But no one has ever dismissed this enchanted island as the Newark of the North. Even President Calvin Coolidge, who was known as "Silent Cal," was moved to

Madeline Island as
seen from Bayfield
Photo by Grandon Harris

fabulous potential wealth in the area was out, and the door would be forever open. In 1665 the missionary Father Claude Allouez left Quebec for Chequamegon Bay escorted by six traders and a large number of Indians—most of whom dropped out along the way—and found villages of Ottawa and Huron Indians upon his arrival.

To say they were unreceptive to his religious efforts would be an understatement; Allouez barely escaped with his life when some angry Indians burned his chapel, and so he returned to Quebec, in his flight becoming the first European to circumnavigate Lake Superior. Father Jacques Marquette had only slightly better results when he resumed mission work in 1669, but he was soon forced to leave as well due to hostilities from Sioux Indians.

Elizabeth Baker and Anne Ashley gathering raspberries on the road to Grant's Point on Madeline Island, about 1913

WHi Image ID 47361

In 1693 a detail of soldiers commanded by Pierre Le Sueur built a fort at the southern end of Madeline Island in a place now known as Grant's Point. The fur trade took off, so much so that a glut a few years later prompted the fort to be abandoned. But other posts would follow in the next century, including one not far from Le Sueur's earlier fort, founded in 1793 by Michel Cadotte for the North West Company. A large boulder and marker now identify the spot on aptly named Old Fort Road heading to Grant's Point.

It was Cadotte who brought romance to the island's story, because if Madeline Island's naming had been an Elizabethan play Michel Cadotte would have been its Romeo and Madeline its Juliet, though luckily their story had no tragic ending. He fell for, and received permission to marry, Ikwesewe, daughter of an important chief named

Wabadjidjak of the White Crane clan. She was baptized at the time of their wedding and given the name Madeleine (the spelling was later changed slightly), a name that Wabadjidjak also decreed for the island itself. From Cadotte's arrival forward La Pointe would be a permanent settlement.

The fur trade would continue for decades. John Jacob Astor's American Fur Company became the major player in the Chequamegon region after 1816, and La Pointe began to resemble a thriving community. A schoolteacher arrived in 1830, and missionary efforts resumed a short time later upon the arrival of Reverend Sherman Hall, the first Protestant minister sent to Wisconsin. A few years later, Father Frederick Baraga established the first permanent Catholic mission on Madeline Island. During this same period, the village of La Pointe was moved to its current location, away from the strong winds that had been experienced on the southeastern tip.

But as Bayfield would later learn time and again, even the richest resources can have limited shelf lives. By 1835 the fur trade was in decline and would continue to decrease in importance; for a time the fur company also engaged in commercial fishing but the diversification did not keep it solvent. It failed in 1845. In the 1850 census, the island's population was put at 485. Ross noted that the census taker had trouble spelling many of the French names but that forty residents were Cadottes, a name still common in Bayfield and the region today.

From left: Genevieve Cadotte La Rush, born on Madeline Island in 1824, daughter of Michel Cadotte Jr., eldest granddaughter of Michel and Madeline Cadotte; Susie Cadotte (or Bazha or Bejig), born in 1833, daughter of Michel Cadotte Jr., holding Joe Cadotte; Angelique (Shibatigokwe), wife of John Cadotte, daughter-in-law of Michel Cadotte Jr. Cadotte is still a common name in the Bayfield region today. Photo courtesy of the National Park Service

Islanders rejoice when inspectors declare the ice road open for travel between La Pointe and Bayfield.
Photo by Don Albrecht

The biggest event of the year on Madeline is the Fourth of July parade, when thousands catch the ferry from Bayfield to stand should-to-shoulder on the main street to applaud, or sometimes laugh at, family floats and funny floats, pick-up marching bands, bicycles, dogs, and children bedecked in red, white, and blue. At the parade's conclusion, the American flag is raised above the fortlike log wall at the museum and freedom is celebrated in word and song, followed by brats in the park, baseball, for some a nap, and, when dark finally descends on a long summer's day, fireworks exploding over the city of La Pointe.

The house that went through the ice in January 1977 made headlines around the world.
Photo courtesy of Roland "Rocky" Barker

When winter stops the ferry in its tracks, conditions can be challenging. Life assumes a slower pace, but with their requisite and resilient make-lemonade spirit, islanders play broomball on the ice or hold car races on the frozen bay's slick surface. Riding a wind sled over ice not safe enough to drive cars and trucks on can be uncomfortable, unsettling, and noisy, which is why islanders rejoice when inspectors declare the ice road open for travel between La Pointe and Bayfield. *The Island Gazette* once called that period "those precious few weeks when us Islanders are not bound to any boat, sled or schedule and can run to Bayfield or Ashland at will and with ease (and best of all for free)." But ice is fickle and ice roads can be fleeting. In 1990 the ice road was open a record eighty-five days, but in recent years seasons of two weeks or less were recorded, and twice now, most recently the winter of 2011–12, conditions were so benign the ferry never stopped running.

Rare is the islander who cannot share a near-death experience of trying to challenge a softening road, and if dropping the occasional car or truck through a weak spot on the ice is not dramatic enough evidence of the ice road's unpredictability, how about dropping a house through? The island made headlines around the world when movers attempting to relocate a two-story house from the mainland to La Pointe in the cold month of January 1977 lost it to weak ice instead. Luckily for folly's record, photographs were taken of the seven-room, fully furnished house as it broke through and slowly sank to the bottom of Lake Superior, and so the image ran in newspapers across the country. And, just like the ill-fated *Edmund Fitzgerald*, the wreck of the house inspired a song: "It Sunk."

If winter's challenges are inevitable, though, so is the arrival of spring and the first wave of tourists coming to experience the same beauty that the long-ago first visitor was moved to record. As Hamilton Ross put it more than a half century ago:

"Although the forests of Madeline Island and the Bayfield peninsula are gone; although the fishing boats, with their quaint sails and sturdy hulls, have been replaced by busy and clamorous gasoline or diesel craft, and although the lumber hookers, with all sail set, no longer pass our door, yet these inroads of so-called civilization cannot rob the region of its glorious sunsets; cannot lessen the mysterious animation and chromatism of the Aurora Borealis; cannot fade the reddish cliffs with their cappings of greenery, nor diminish the unparalleled blueness of the lake.

"Neither can they take away the fairy land of autumnal foliage or the experience of cruising along the beaches and into the wave-worn caves of the headlands in a small boat, and drinking in their ineffable charm and beauty. Like Michel Cadotte, we may still gaze at the play of shadows on the opposite hills, and watch the ever-changing colors of the lake."

Idyllic, yes. Stick to that.

Big Bay State Park on Madeline Island was established in 1963 to provide an area for outdoor recreation and to educate the public about nature and conservation. Park development began in 1967, and today the park offers visitors a beach, a campground, picnic areas, and more than seven miles of hiking and nature trails.

Photo by Grandon Harris

THE FERRY

It might not occur to many first-time visitors to Madeline Island, but those who look back into the past instead of ahead at the lovely island they are approaching will understand that they are following in the paddle prints of the Ojibwe who made the same crossing centuries earlier and in the wake of all manner of differently powered watercraft that followed. They are, in fact, already experiencing the heritage of island life before they even step foot on its approaching landing.

The Madeline Island Ferry Line has dependably carried fun-seekers, school-children, construction workers, and all the niceties and necessities of life since it was born in the merger of two competing ferry lines in 1970. But the not-always-so-easy task of getting from here to there—and of course from there to here again—has been a critically important pursuit on Chequamegon Bay since the earliest days of human activity.

The Ojibwe who made their home on Madeline Island at the time French traders

In 1970 two competing ferry owners joined their operations to create the Madeline Island Ferry Line, and today the distinctive blue-and-white vessels are an integral element of the local waterscape.
Photo by Don Albrecht

THE FERRY

and explorers reached the bay relied on birch bark canoes to fish the waters of Lake Superior or to go to the mainland to hunt or gather food. Trade for furs and other goods similarly depended upon water connections, and as rough communities began to appear at Ashland, Bayfield, Washburn, and elsewhere on the lake, commercial water transportation became the preferred mode of getting around. Even when early roads were developed, travel by water was often more comfortable and reliable than braving rough and rutted land routes.

Early ferries, and there were many, were usually small sailboats or rowboats. Not much is known of them, but a ferry boat history prepared for the Madeline Island Ferry Line by the Madeline Island Museum's Sheree Peterson noted that some forty mechanically powered ferries have been documented as having carried freight and passengers on Chequamegon Bay.

As early as 1870, the steamer *Minnie V.* made more than three hundred trips from her home in

Bayfield to La Pointe, Ashland, Red Cliff, and Apostle Island destinations. Other craft soon joined the business, especially after the arrival of the railroad increased both passenger traffic and commercial enterprises in the region. Peterson said the Wisconsin Central railway, for example, arrived daily in Ashland while offering a connection to Bayfield on "the elegant steam ferry *S.B. Barker*," which boasted room for as many as 350 passengers. Later came the tug *Cora Fuller*, the steam yacht *Waubun*, the

(continued on next page)

In 1939, the Russell brothers' ferry line (which would eventually merge with Harry Nelson's competing line) acquired a ferry with a two-car capacity. Named the *Gar-How* after Howard Russell's sons, Gary and Howard, the boat was built at La Pointe by Emil Erickson and August Wick. The *Gar-How* spent her last days in the Reiten boatyard in Bayfield.
Photo courtesy of the National Park Service

8 In the Ancient Apostles, a Park Is Born

The Apostle Islands National Lakeshore has been a reality since 1970, so long that many in the army of largely young kayakers, campers, hikers, and boaters who come from afar to play within its boundaries may think it has always served as a park for pleasure.

Not so. Those with longer memories, especially among the residents of communities along the Lake Superior shoreline, remember well that before they were reserved for recreation, the islands were worked hard, lived upon, and sometimes privately owned, and, even more, that establishing a national park on the island-dotted edge of the Bayfield peninsula was no easy task. In fact, it took almost a decade for park champion Gaylord Nelson's national lakeshore proposal to become reality, and another sixteen years to add the final piece, Long Island, to the park that now includes twenty-one of the Apostle Islands—all but Madeline—and twelve miles of mainland lakeshore. And all of that only came decades after earlier proposals to create either state or national parks in the Apostle Islands went nowhere.

As early as 1891, the *Ashland Daily Press* had urged creation of a national park for the Apostle Islands. The earliest real effort to accomplish that came in the late 1920s, when local officials began seeing tourism as the obvious replacement for the fading lumber industry. A national park, especially, was seen as a lure that would bring thousands of people to far northern Wisconsin, a place not on many tourist itineraries at the time. And such a proposal dovetailed nicely with concerns that the islands would be bought up and controlled by wealthy interests and thus off limits to the masses.

The first plan for a park included Madeline Island and several others, but when a National Park Service official came to Chequamegon Bay to inspect the area's suitability for a park he was less than impressed. The islands still bore the scars of lumbering and did not at all look like the leafy paradise visitors find today. After two days touring

A kayaker paddles by the mainland sea caves near Meyers Beach. Even seasoned paddlers are warned to watch for changing weather because, as local T-shirts remind, "The Lake Is the Boss."
Photo courtesy of the National Park Service

Less than two months later, Kennedy was killed in Dallas. And while it took years for the final plan to clear every bureaucratic and political hurdle, President Richard Nixon in 1970 finally signed a bill establishing the Apostle Islands National Lakeshore. In 1986 Long Island, which had been excluded from the original lakeshore because of earlier opposition from Bad River officials, was added to the park. Madeline Island, because of its large amount of privately owned land, permanent residents, extensive road system, and the presence of Big Bay State Park, was excluded from the national lakeshore.

In 2004 another significant step was taken when President George W. Bush signed a bill designating that 80 percent of the land area of the Apostle Islands National Lakeshore be managed as federally protected wilderness. Appropriately, it was named the Gaylord Nelson Wilderness, honoring the man who more than any other helped the dream become reality. Nelson's daughter, Tia, was on hand for the dedication.

And that latest step deserves applause today just as it did on the day the park was finally approved. The park today draws tens of thousands of visitors to Wisconsin's northern tip, an average of more than 172,000 annually in recent years. A study

Though the islands are largely managed as wilderness, some human footprints are still visible to lakeshore visitors today, such as this vehicle left behind on Sand Island.
Photo courtesy of the National Park Service

Excursion boat *Apostle Islands*, operated by Booth Fisheries Corporation, tying up at Sand Island, 1940s

Photo courtesy of the National Park Service

conducted a few years ago listed sightseeing as the most popular activity, followed by walking the beaches, taking photographs, hiking, visiting exhibits at visitor centers, and on through more than a dozen other activities.

Though the islands are largely managed as wilderness, some human footprints are still visible to lakeshore visitors today, from such obvious structures as lighthouses that once were homes to keepers and their families to old sandstone quarries and the remnants of once-managed orchards. Visitors will also find camping sites, hiking trails, docks for sail and power boats to tie up to, and, on Stockton Island, the most visited of the Apostles, a ranger station where interpretive programs and other activities take place.

Similarly, visitors today can find ample examples of the kinds of activities that once made the islands such a vibrant part of Chequamegon life and labor. The Apostle Islands National Lakeshore Visitor Center, the first stop for visitors making their initial exploration of the islands, is housed in the Old County Courthouse in Bayfield, constructed of the very brownstone blocks once quarried both among the islands and on the mainland.

The Apostle Islands National Lakeshore Visitor Center in Bayfield has historical displays, including an exhibit on the Fresnel lens that revolutionized the work of lighthouses and their keepers, along with books and videos on the Apostle Islands, the Great Lakes, and more. Information on camping and visiting the islands is also available at the visitor center.

Additional information on the national lakeshore can be found at another visitor center at Little Sand Bay, thirteen miles north of Bayfield. Here the National Park Service maintains Hokenson Brothers Fishery, a historic family commercial fishing site begun in 1927 by three brothers who turned to the lake for a living after farming failed them. The site, listed on the National Register of Historic Places, includes fishery buildings and equipment along with the dock they used for their homemade tug, *Trawler*.

The Park Service also maintains the Manitou Island Fish Camp, where volunteers in summer will take visitors into the rough cabin and other buildings that represent how commercial fishermen lived and worked in the heyday of the industry. For some, any romantic notions of life as a commercial fisherman will be erased by the rustic conditions depicted by volunteers who live in the camp each summer, while others who find

9 Agriculture's Roots Take Hold

The earliest efforts to lure settlers to the Chequamegon region emphasized the natural beauty of the area as well as the fine harbor that was surely destined to make Bayfield the Chicago of the far north. And given the dreams of land ownership and self-sufficiency held by many who considered starting a new life on the new frontier, these pitches to prospective settlers also hit hard on the ease with which agriculture could be practiced, the availability of land for any and all comers, and growing conditions that would rival any in the world. Declaring in printed appeals to settlers that "We can beat old Ireland in size and quality of potatoes" surely must have whetted the appetites of would-be growers everywhere.

Of course, such blue-sky come-ons neglected to point out that much of the land was covered by forest, or riddled with rocks and stumps from forests that had been felled, or that land in the northern reaches of Wisconsin came with a short growing season—and that some of the lands were on islands, a choppy boat ride from the mainland. Dreams were dreams, though, and early residents went into the fields with the unbridled optimism such a fickle business as farming demanded.

It was not that the region lacked assets important to agriculture. Unlike areas to the south, the Chequamegon area offered a system

Hay mower with Jake Hansen, on Sand Island. The horse's name was Bob.
Photo courtesy of the National Park Service, from the Alma Hansen Dahl collection

Blue Vista Farm, Bayfield
Photo by Grandon Harris

of water transport that would allow products to be efficiently sent to market. And while clearing land could be a challenge, the glacially formed soils in the area were suitable for fruits, vegetables, and small grains.

The most significant blessing came from the great lake itself, and the so-called lake effect. Along Bayfield's shoreline, surface water that warms during the summer and early fall retains heat well into autumn, delaying the arrival of the first killing frost and thus extending the growing season. In "Farming the Lake Superior Shore," an examination of agriculture and horticulture in the Apostle Islands published in the *Wisconsin Magazine of History*, writers Alan R. Alanen and William Tishler noted that despite the region's northern situation, climatologists believed the growing season equaled that in areas hundreds of miles to the south.

Small-scale farming had taken place even before the city of Bayfield was founded and began seeking settlers. Native Americans had grown crops, and the French fur traders had maintained gardens for personal use on Madeline Island. Alanen and Tishler noted that William Wilson, the hermit who gave Hermit Island its fanciful name, had kept a garden there and sold vegetables on his rare trips to the mainland. Ojibwe families long were engaged in blueberry picking, both for personal consumption and to sell in nearby communities. There were also several attempts in the 1860s and 1870s to develop orchards on some islands. A Civil War veteran named Richard McCloud

the fruit business, as it remains today. By 1910 growers had formed the Bayfield Fruit Association to help with marketing, and that organization later became a co-op that served growers' needs for many years, shipping fruit by rail from its headquarters on the edge of the lake.

Tasty evidence that Knight knew what he was doing can be found yet today in Bayfield's orchard district, where some of his original trees are still producing apples at Hauser's Superior View Farm. John Hauser, who had studied horticulture at the University of Wisconsin and worked for a seed company, came to Bayfield with his family in 1908. He grew strawberries and potatoes, among other endeavors, but when an embargo was placed on seeds from Europe in 1912 he saw opportunity in growing and selling perennial plants in addition to producing fruit. Both pursuits continue today; in addition to selling plants for local gardeners, the Hauser family, now in the fifth generation of involvement, ships all across the country in spring and fall.

The Superior view that gave its name to the family farm is best observed from the window of Hauser's large red barn, which is itself a pretty good tale of a simpler time. The barn, made of western fir, was ordered from the famed Sears, Roebuck and Co. catalog, shipped by rail from the west, hauled up the steep hill to the orchard district on horse-drawn wagons, and assembled by local carpenters. A page from the catalog now

South Shore Farm, located on one of the Apostle Islands, ca. 1910. This image is part of the Elizabeth Abernathy Hull collection. Hull was raised in the Kansas City area. She took up the camera as a schoolgirl, photographing family, friends, picnics, boating, berry picking, and summer resort life on Madeline Island, where her family owned Coole Park Manor from 1905 to around 1946.

WHi Image ID 47519

framed in the barn's lower level shows the purchase price for "Modern Barn #2061" was $896.

John Hauser bought some of Knight's trees in 1920, at a time when there were far more apple trees in the orchard district than even today. Jim Hauser Jr., John's grandson, said, "Everybody had the idea they could make money growing apples."

As is often the case with farming, producing goods was often easier than selling them for a profit. By the 1950s, many orchard owners had their own trucks that they used to deliver apples throughout Wisconsin and neighboring states, and it was on one such mission that the modern-day Apple Festival, often counted among the premier community festivals anywhere in the Midwest, was conceived.

James Erickson, who was both a commercial fisherman and an orchard owner, recalled that around 1961 he was delivering a truckload of apples when his truck suffered a flat tire near Duluth. To compound that misfortune, Erickson had left home without a spare tire. As he explained some fifty years later, "I forgot it."

But while he sat on the side of the road waiting for a tire to be delivered, the "Erickson Orchard" sign on the side of his truck drew attention—as did the bushels of ripe and red apples in the truck's open back. Ever the promoter, Erickson took advantage of that.

"I sold twenty bushels of apples out of the truck," he recalled, but what made an even bigger impression on him was that so many of his new customers did not seem to know where Bayfield was, even though it was just seventy-five miles to the east.

Something, he said to himself, should be done about that. Soon after, Erickson was part of a local committee looking for ways to extend the fall tourism season. He described his experience and suggested an apple festival that would introduce the world, or at least a few thousand people a year, to Bayfield.

It was not that the festival idea was new to the city. Years before Bayfield had held strawberry festivals, and in the 1950s several fall festivals featured apples and their many uses, to only

Even though Bayfield is so far north, the lake effect produces a climate perfectly suited to growing apples.
Photo by Doug Alft, courtesy of the Wisconsin Department of Tourism

Bayfield's Apple Festival in October regularly draws crowds in the tens of thousands, despite weather that can range from warm and sunny one year to snow flurries another. It is always Bayfield's busiest weekend and a fun way to celebrate the apple harvest.

Photo by Grandon Harris

modest success. In Jim Erickson's more blunt assessment, "It fell flat on its face," in large part because farmers—already at their busiest time of the year—were in charge. The new Apple Festival he proposed to the committee was put under the auspices of the Chamber of Commerce, where it prospered.

Apples are hardly the only fruit grown in Bayfield's hilly orchard district, though. Local residents impatiently await the seasonal progression from strawberries in late June and early July to raspberries, cherries, blueberries, and blackberries later in the summer, along with a wide variety of fresh and organic vegetables grown on area farms. Hungry visitors come from far and wide to pick their own berries or buy flats of ready-to-eats. In addition, some orchards and farms offer everything from pears, grapes, dried flowers, and honey to farm-made jams and jellies, cider, and even wine.

But that is all build-up to the first full weekend of October and Apple Festival, come rain, shine, or occasional snow showers. The city's fiftieth Apple Festival was celebrated in 2011, a three-day blowout of food, music, entertainment, and all things remotely apple. Now when the festival finds good weather it draws tens of thousands of visitors from throughout Wisconsin and the Midwest, but the celebration took some time to grow so big. The 1962 festival, the first to feature a queen, brought about four thousand visitors to Bayfield, and similar crowds attended in following years. But word spread and attendance grew, reaching an estimated eight thousand in 1970, according to Virginia Beauchamp's history of the event, and ten thousand the following year.

By the end of the decade, attendance was estimated at twenty-five thousand, and as Bayfield's Apple Festival began getting national publicity in travel publications and rankings on "best festival" lists, the event continued to get bigger. Traditions now include the popular apple pie baking contest, the appearance of the pipe and drum group from Thunder Bay, Ontario, and the "mass band" that brings up the rear of Sunday's closing parade, featuring the members of all the marching bands from the parade making one more noisy pass through the crowd.

Apple Festival serves as more than a community celebration and economic boost, though it is certainly important on both counts. Fritz Hauser, the fourth-generation owner of John Hauser's original orchard, said several areas of Wisconsin produce more apples than Bayfield does and, with more southerly locations, have them ready for market sooner. Because of Apple Festival, however, many think of Bayfield as the state's apple capital and, just as important, the hungry crowds that head north eliminate the need to truck apples far and wide. "Applefest plays a big part [in marketing]," he said, "because it gets people to come here."

Just one more benefit of the wholesome apple.

10 A Journey, a Struggle, a Home

While Bayfield is often viewed as part of the three-community shoreline cluster that also includes Washburn and Ashland—Mount Ashwabay, which takes its name from the three, is only the most obvious example of that conflation—its closest neighbor actually lies on the other side of the Bayfield peninsula. The Red Cliff Band of Lake Superior Chippewa, whose name derives from the red stone banks along the shore of Chequamegon Bay where their reservation hugs the water, have made their homes just three miles north of Bayfield since about the time the city itself was established.

Before that they were residents of Madeline Island. And the traditional story of how the Ojibwe came to the place they called "the home of the golden-breasted woodpecker" is richer and more colorful than any two-men-and-a-canoe discovery story that later white explorers could share.

The migration story was one of a number of oral traditions passed down through the years. As it begins, the Anishinaabe, usually defined as first or original people, were living along the eastern coast of North America with many other native groups that included the Ottawa and Potawatomi. They lived in such numbers, wrote Edward Benton-Banai, a spiritual leader of the Lac Courte Oreilles Band of Ojibwe, "that if one was to climb the highest mountain and look in all directions, they would not be able to see the end of the nation."

One of the first written versions of the story was by William Warren, the son of a white man and an Ojibwe woman, whose *History of the Ojibwe People*, published in 1885, is widely viewed as the most important history of the tribe ever written. Based on the oral accounts of tribal elders, Warren described how the Anishinaabe began migrating west, heeding the prophecies of the Seven Fires that a move was necessary to protect their traditional culture. They were to follow a sacred Megis shell that would take them to seven stopping places before finally discovering the "food that grows on water."

Ojibwe dancers from both the Bad River and Red Cliff reservations performed at Bayfield's Apple Fest in 2009.
Photo by Don Albrecht

One of their stopping places was "the place of the Thunder Water," or Niagara Falls, and another was Sault Sainte Marie. Along the way the group divided responsibilities; the Potawatomi were in charge of keeping the sacred fire, the Ottawa were to provide food and supplies for all the nation, and the Ojibwe were the faith keepers, entrusted with the sacred scrolls and drum of the Midewiwin, or medicine society.

The sixth stopping place was Spirit Island, or modern-day Duluth. It was along the southern shore of Lake Superior that they also found the "food that grows on water," or wild rice. And it was nearby that they came to the seventh and final stopping place, the turtle-shaped island that had been foretold.

That is why, Warren wrote, tribal members would often say in their speeches that La Pointe was "the spot on which the Ojibwe tribe first grew, and like a tree has spread its branches in every direction, in the bands that now occupy the vast extent of the Ojibwe earth." The island would, of course, later be named Madeline Island when the eldest daughter of White Crane, hereditary chief of the Crane Clan, married the French fur trader Michel Cadotte. Beyond serving as their physical home, the island became a sacred center for the Ojibwe people.

The Ojibwe got along well with the French traders, who were eager to exchange modern goods for the furs they coveted. There was much intermarriage, and the Indians were willing allies of the French in their ongoing disputes with the British. According to *Indian Nations of Wisconsin* by Patty Loew, a member of the Bad River Band, former public television host, and professor at the University of Wisconsin–Madison, the Ojibwe also used the guns they had acquired from the French in their own ongoing battles with the Dakota, their fiercest rivals, over the control of wild rice beds.

For a long time, the Ojibwe lived off the land in traditional ways, gathering nuts and berries, making maple syrup, fishing the waters of Lake Superior, hunting, gardening, and of course harvesting wild rice. In time, however, the federal government's interest in westward expansion led to the forced removal of many Indian tribes, and the Ojibwe were inevitably caught in the crosshairs of those policies. In treaties enacted in 1837 and 1842, the Ojibwe ceded to the government millions of acres of land, including the magnificent and then largely untouched pine and hardwood forests that spread across most of northern Wisconsin, Minnesota, and Michigan's Upper Peninsula.

PICTOGRAPH. A.   Pl. 60

SYMBOLIC PETITION OF CHIPPEWA CHIEFS,
presented at Washington, January 28th 1849, headed by Oshcabawis of Monomonecau, Wisconsin.

As described in Patty Loew's book *Indian Nations of Wisconsin: Histories of Endurance and Renewal*, this is an artist's copy of a nineteenth-century petition, created on birch bark, from Ojibwe clan chiefs. The animal figures represent clan leaders, the thick line represents Lake Superior, and the four small ovals represent the rice beds. This petition indicates that the Ojibwe are united in their wish not to be removed from their wild rice beds near Lake Superior.
WHi Image ID 1871

Importantly, though, in both treaties the Ojibwe retained their traditional rights to hunt, fish, and gather on those ceded lands, a move that more than a century later would lead to a protracted legal battle over such rights and widespread protests across the north when the Ojibwe prevailed.

The treaties had assured the Ojibwe that as long as there were no hostilities with white settlers they would be allowed to stay on their land. But just a few years later, the government attempted to move the Ojibwe to Minnesota, where officials had their eyes on the annuity money and federal funds awarded for Indian schools and other facilities. In 1850 President Zachary Taylor ordered the Ojibwe to move west of the Mississippi River, but the order was met by widespread opposition from both Indian and white interests.

Still, in October of that year the Office of Indian Affairs decreed that tribal members would have to travel to Sandy Lake, Minnesota, to collect their annuities instead of receiving them as usual on Madeline Island, their spiritual home. Alexander Ramsay, the Superintendent of Indian Affairs in Minnesota, and other officials thought that if the Ojibwe spent the winter at Sandy Lake because of oncoming weather they might yet be persuaded to take up permanent residence and, in so doing, bring federal money to the region.

Instead, the move proved to be a tragic and deadly debacle. When the Ojibwe reached Sandy Lake they found food in short supply even as a harsh winter was already setting in. Conditions grew desperate, and the rations offered by government workers were of such poor quality as to be often inedible. Disease followed the hunger, and ultimately more than 150 Ojibwa died at Sandy Lake and many more during their desperate efforts to return to their homes.

One of the most eloquent voices of the suffering Ojibwe was that of Chief Buffalo, who lived at La Pointe. Despite advanced age—he was in his nineties—Chief Buffalo and other leaders fought the removal order, pleading, as he did in an 1851 letter, to "be permitted to remain here where we were promised we might live, as long as we were not in the way of the Whites," Loew reported. More than not being in the way of whites, Buffalo argued, the Ojibwe had not engaged in any hostilities that would have voided their agreements.

As Larry Balber, Red Cliff's historic preservation officer, wryly described the situation more than 150 years later, "The French came, they left. The British came, they left. The Americans came, now we got to leave. But our creation stories, our migration stories, tell us there is no other place for us [than Chequamegon Bay]."

In 1852 Chief Buffalo took more direct action, journeying for some ten weeks from Madeline Island to Washington, DC, to plead his people's case. The white interpreter Benjamin Armstrong and other hereditary leaders joined Chief Buffalo, then ninety-two; along the way the group made a number of stops to gather signatures on

Grandson of Great Chief Buffalo. Chief Buffalo was a principal chief of the Lake Superior Band of Ojibwe. He was also known as Ke-che-waish-ke (Great Renewer), Peezhickee or Bishiki (Buffalo), and (in French) Le Beouf. He was born at La Pointe on Madeline Island in about 1759 and died September 7, 1855, at La Pointe.

WHi Image ID 3957

a petition supporting their cause. Their path took them through the Great Lakes, eventually to Buffalo, and then by train to Albany, where they boarded a steamer that sailed to New York City, their last stop before Washington.

Initially, the group was told they had no invitation and instead should return home. But a New York congressman and several members of President Millard Fillmore's staff came by chance into contact with the delegation while dining and helped arrange a meeting with the president. The following day, Chief Buffalo opened the meeting with a traditional pipe ceremony, and after everyone had smoked the group made their case. Several days later, President Fillmore called them back to the White House to say the removal order would be dropped and annuity payments would again be made at La Pointe instead of in Minnesota.

In 1854 another treaty was made between the Ojibwe and the federal government, again with Benjamin Armstrong on hand to represent the Ojibwe. As a result of this treaty, the Ojibwe established four reservations—at Bad River east of Ashland, Lac Courte Oreilles near Hayward in Sawyer County, Lac du Flambeau near Minocqua in Vilas County, and at Red Cliff. Again, the Ojibwe specifically reserved the right to hunt, fish, and gather on ceded lands. Chief Buffalo and his family, along with other Ojibwe who had converted to Christianity, moved from La Pointe to Red Cliff, near their traditional fishing grounds, while a larger number of Ojibwe moved to the Bad River Reservation at Odanah, where there were extensive wild rice beds. In 1863 the Red Cliff Reservation was expanded to fourteen thousand acres.

For residents of Red Cliff, as was true in many other native communities, being granted reservations and a limited form of sovereign government status did little to end the challenges of coexisting with the larger and financially controlling white world. Federal policies ranging from Indian boarding schools to allotments of individually owned land were aimed at "civilizing" the natives but instead led to the further degradation of traditional life and culture. Many impoverished Indians sold their land to white buyers because they were desperate for income or lost it for their inability to pay property taxes.

Many Ojibwe men took jobs in the forests or, later, as commercial fishermen. Red Cliff had its own sawmill for a time, but after it burned down it was not rebuilt, and eventually the lumbering era passed for everyone. Some on the reservation practiced small-scale farming, but they had limited commercial success.

"By 1929," Loew wrote, "few Red Cliff Ojibwe even felt the effects of the Great Depression. Their economy had already been depressed for years. Ninety-five percent of tribal members had sold or lost their land to foreclosures."

For economic reasons, many Ojibwe across northern Wisconsin left reservations to look for work in large cities such as Milwaukee, Chicago, and the Twin Cities. In addition, many Ojibwe men, while legally part of a separate and sovereign nation, enlisted in the military in numbers disproportionate to their tribal populations, serving in both world wars, the Korean War, and later in the Vietnam War. "We became citizens [of the United States] in 1924," Balber said, "but even prior to that we were serving in the military."

Eventually, government policies that took Indian children off of reservations to attend boarding schools and other assimilation programs were ended. But even as native communities began to form new government structures and regain some form of self-government, life on the reservations continued to pose daunting challenges, Balber said.

"A lot of things that made life sustainable became difficult," he said. "And there were choices made. Some couldn't wait to get out, and some were taken and a day later packed their bags and started walking home."

Annuity payment at La Pointe, on Madeline Island. Seated on the right is John W. Bell. Others are, left to right, Asaph Whittlesey, Agent Henry C. Gilbert, and William S. Warren.

WHi Image ID 48581

Always there was the difficulty of living as Indian in a much larger dominant culture. In the late 1960s and 1970s, at the same time that the antiwar movement, the women's movement, and other political upheavals were changing American life, the so-called Red Power movement prompted many Native American communities to begin asserting themselves more and demanding that they be allowed to exercise rights they had reserved but that government policies had forbidden them to enjoy.

One of those rights was harvesting fish, including by spearing during the spring spawning season, off the reservation but on ceded lands. In 1974, two Ojibwe brothers allowed themselves to be arrested while ice fishing in such a manner, setting off a legal fight that would last more than a decade. Five Ojibwe bands became part of the lawsuit, and in 1983 the final court's action upheld the right to fish, hunt, and gather under terms of those earlier treaties.

The foresight of their forefathers had been affirmed. Yet the legal ruling did little to stifle resentment among many white residents of Wisconsin, and especially during the spring spawning season tribal spear fishermen were met with noisy protests and threats of violence—and sometimes rock throwing and other physical confrontations—that necessitated a heavy police presence on northern boat landings. Eventually, court injunctions helped to quiet most of the protests, and concerns that spearing spawning female walleyes would decimate fish populations on lakes popular with sport fishermen were addressed by the creation of the Great Lakes Indian Fish and Wildlife Commission, whose wardens and biologists work with the Wisconsin Department of Natural Resources to monitor treaty fishing and hunting. The commission is based at Odanah, on the Bad River Reservation, but some Red Cliff residents are employed there as well. In addition, the Red Cliff tribal fish hatchery supplies eggs, fry, and fish for both on- and off-reservation stocking, working in conjunction with state and federal agencies.

Ojibwe man, Red Cliff powwow, ca. 1913, photo by Elizabeth Hull. In her recollections of attending the summer Red Cliff powwow, Elizabeth Hull mentions purchasing two beaded items from this gentleman, both of which she donated to the Madeline Island Museum in 1961.
WHi Image ID 52830

Bead appliqué on velveteen/cotton, Ojibwe, ca. 1900–1910 (43 by 14.75 inches). This is the largest and most exquisite bag in the Madeline Island Museum's collection.

Madeline Island Museum #83.237.558, photo by Mark Fay

The treaty rights battle was a victory not only because it affirmed the earlier reserved rights, in Balber's view, but also for how it helped preserve tribal identity. In a sense, the tribes were fighting for their rights just as Chief Buffalo had earlier fought for their land.

Another link to Chief Buffalo was realized in 2010 with the return to the Red Cliff tribe of the pipe that Chief Buffalo and his party had carried to Washington in 1852. The pipe, about four feet long and made in two pieces, was created specifically for the journey, Balber said, and became a key part of setting the tone at the meeting between Chief Buffalo's party and President Fillmore. When the meeting opened, Chief Buffalo asked that all present first smoke the pipe of peace, according to a later account by his interpreter, Benjamin Armstrong, and even the president took "two or three draughts from it."

Later, Chief Buffalo presented the pipe to Armstrong, who was not only a good friend of the Red Cliff Ojibwe but who had also married into Chief Buffalo's family. Armstrong kept it until passing it on to his son, and it stayed in the family until, in 2010, Dan Brown, the great-great-great-grandson of Chief Buffalo, offered to return it to the Red Cliff.

The pipe's significance to the Ojibwe at Red Cliff goes beyond historical artifact, Balber said, because it also represents "peace, homelands and maintaining our life here, forever. We had to fight to protect [our homeland]. That was part of what was carried in that pipe, that we were prepared to defend it."

In the end, the pipe of peace brought peace, instead. And it is one of a number of historical artifacts the tribe is considering ways to preserve, just as it is struggling to keep its traditional language and other cultural traditions alive. Today there are only a few fluent language speakers, Balber said, and the job of preserving cultural identity in a dominant white society comes "with difficulty. It's a struggle. It's a struggle that continually persists."

Like so many other Indian communities, the Red Cliff Band has turned to gaming to boost employment on the reservation and to fund tribal programs for housing, elder care, transportation, and other needs. Until 2011 Red Cliff's Isle Vista Casino was small and generated far less traffic than larger casinos like those at Bad River, on busy Highway 2, or Lac Courte Oreilles, near the more populous Hayward area. But in 2011,

Legendary Waters Resort & Casino, sited on land owned by the Red Cliff Band of Lake Superior Ojibwe, overlooks the Apostle Islands National Lakeshore.
Photo courtesy of Legendary Waters Resort & Casino

Legendary Waters Resort & Casino opened at Red Cliff, overlooking the waters of Chequamegon Bay. In addition to the casino, the property includes a hotel, restaurant, and conference center, which tribal officials hope will spur the reservation economy by creating jobs and opportunities.

In addition, in 2011 the Red Cliff tribe, working with the Bayfield Regional Conservancy and federal agencies, were successful in buying eighty-eight acres of shoreline and forestland at Frog Bay on the reservation. Frog Bay Tribal National Park opened to the public in August 2012. Its purpose, like that of the larger Apostle Islands National Lakeshore that surrounds it, is to help further preserve the homeland the Ojibwe were led to by the Megis shell so long ago.

11 Rooms with a View

It was only logical that, as enticing as Bayfield and the Apostle Islands were to hardworking settlers in the region's early years, the clean air, breathtaking sunsets, and wondrous meetings of soaring red bluffs and deep blue water would hold even more allure for visitors seeking relaxation or recreation. According to Hamilton Nelson Ross's account of Madeline Island history, as early as 1854, even before Bayfield was formally established, the *New York Daily Tribune* saw the area's potential for summer tourism, noting, "This is certainly the most delightful situation in Lake Superior."

Accommodations for travelers abound in Bayfield, from cozy guest rooms in historic buildings to modern hotels, motels, apartments, and condos, with all manner of cottages, cabins, B&Bs, lodges, and resorts in between.
Photo by Grandon Harris

One visitor who came to sample the region's summer delights in 1868 was none other than Mrs. Abraham Lincoln, whose tour included a visit to La Pointe. Of course, La Pointe then was not as ready for tourists as La Pointe today, and Mrs. Lincoln was pointedly warned, "Don't stay at the Cramer hotel whatever you do; it's full of knot holes and the men snore something awful."

The former first lady, it should be noted, spent her day on the island but her night on the mainland. Still, today's island visitor who is kept awake at night by bar-time music from certain La Pointe establishments should know that it could be worse: the next room could have been rented by noisily snoring lumberjacks.

Early lodging choices for visitors were mostly rustic boardinghouses, but then the area was largely still newly settled frontier. Several boardinghouses and small hotels were available on Madeline Island, in Ashland, and in Bayfield, where the Bayfield Exchange Hotel was established shortly after the town was settled. Of course, given the new city's location, any would-be tourist had to arrive by water because travel by road, and more importantly the railroad, was still a future dream.

For much of the city's first century, tourism was just part of a larger economy that included lumbering, fishing, farming, and other activities. But it was always an important part of Bayfield life, and after the opening of the canal at Sault Sainte Marie in 1855 made travel on the Great Lakes easier, a steady stream of steamships brought visitors

THE CHEQUAMEGON, ASHLAND, WIS.

The Chequamegon Hotel in Ashland. Built by the Wisconsin Central Railroad and opened in 1877, it was condemned as a fire trap and razed in the 1890s.
WHi Image ID 3816

The Island View Hotel. Its guests included passengers who arrived in Bayfield on luxurious excursion boats from Buffalo, Detroit, and Chicago. It catered to tourists for only seventeen years, 1883 to 1900, and was razed in 1913.
Photo courtesy of the Bayfield Heritage Association, 1980-34-001

by water to enjoy a Chequamegon summer. In her writings about pioneer Bayfield, newspaper columnist Eleanor Knight noted that 1872 had been a good year for visitors. "Quite a large number of pleasure seekers have been with us this week and our hotels are overflowing." Several bridal parties had chosen Bayfield for their honeymoons, she wrote, and a photographer had set up shop on Fourth Street to take souvenir images of the intrepid tourists.

From the very beginning, the region was hailed as a tonic for hay-fever sufferers, given the clean air and lack of sneeze-inducing plants along the Lake Superior shoreline. And local newspapers, always hometown boosters as much as purveyors of news, were happy to spread the word. Eschewing any semblance of modesty or objectivity, the *Bayfield Press* was quick to offer such praise as, "No place in the country is blessed with purer atmosphere and water, or a more salubrious and delightful climate than Bayfield . . . and it is destined to become one of the greatest resorts for the health and pleasure seeker on the continent." The *Press*, it seems, did not believe in small dreams.

Tourism took on a different dimension with the arrival of the railroad, first the Wisconsin Central line to Ashland in 1877 and, six years later, the Chicago, St. Paul, Minneapolis & Omaha. As the opening of the Sault locks had made boat travel more accessible, the arrival of twin rails made it easier for travelers from Chicago, Milwaukee, and other big cities to reach the Chequamegon area. Then, as today, the region became a popular destination for residents of Minneapolis and St. Paul.

But getting people here was one thing; housing them was another. To encourage leisure travel the railroads established large hotels, first the Hotel Chequamegon in

The intended mission of the Indian Pageant was to interpret Indian life, but in the end the program treated Indians more as novelties than as people whose ancestors, history, and traditions have been established in the Apostle Island region for centuries.
Photo by Gil Larsen, courtesy of the Bayfield Heritage Association

touring northern cities, spent his time trout fishing on the Brule River, where he stayed in a lodge on Cedar Island. One of the places Coolidge and his wife visited was the Apostle Islands, where they enjoyed a tour of the sea caves at Devil's Island and a stop for tea on Madeline Island, where they also toured historic sights.

In the end, Coolidge stayed in Wisconsin for eighty-eight days, even skipping the Republican convention, and left behind an endorsement that would make a Chamber of Commerce director swoon. Superior country, he said presidentially, was "a vigorous, enterprising, growing region and you may well be proud of it." And, he added, "The fishing around here, I can testify, is very excellent."

Fishing, and camping, did become more popular. Sport fishing continued to draw big numbers as the area's reputation as a trollers' paradise spread and charter fishing boat captains formed the Bayfield Trollers Association to promote their industry. Deer hunting was a popular activity among the Apostle Islands in the fall, and camping became more popular, bringing yet another group of outdoor enthusiasts.

The demise of the commercial fishing industry left Bayfield rather adrift economically in the 1950s and '60s. That distress, felt elsewhere in the north as well in that period, gave added impetus to the creation of the Apostle Islands National Lakeshore. While some feared it would change forever the nature of Bayfield and its environs by bringing in ever more tourists to frolic on the water and the islands, others viewed it as the necessary catalyst to make tourism the driving force in the local economy. To count the number of brightly colored kayaks atop cars on Bayfield's downtown streets in summer, or the number of visitors climbing aboard Apostle Islands Cruise Service boats for morning or evening island tours, is to suggest that both sides were right.

A stamp presumably issued by the Outdoor Club of Wisconsin to promote tourism in northern Wisconsin. In 1928 President Calvin Coolidge set up a "summer White House" in Superior, Wisconsin. One of the places he visited was the Apostle Islands.
WHI Image ID 44768

Today tourists come not only for the outdoor recreational possibilities that are constants but also for the work of the many artists who make the Bayfield peninsula their home and for the historic house shows and national touring acts that make Lake Superior Big Top Chautauqua the place to be on a warm summer night. They come for whitefish livers, that oddball local delicacy, and to pick blueberries or strawberries or apples. They come for festivals in summer and dog sledding or snowshoeing in winter, a season that has grown in importance to the local economy. Or they come to simply relax, as Warren Nelson said so well in his iconic song "Over to Old La Pointe": "Nothing to do will do for me, it's what I come here for."

It is also worth noting that, unlike the numbers of fish in Lake Superior or white pine and hemlock in Bayfield County forests, the undeniable beauty that draws visitors by the hundreds of thousands each year will not be exhausted by overuse or excessive appreciation. Care must be taken to protect the environment of Chequamegon Bay and its natural assets, and a number of local and regional organizations are working tirelessly to do so, but Bayfield, and its shoreline neighborhood, remains a place of glittering waters, magnificent sunsets, and beckoning vibe.

Need more proof than your own eyes supply? In 1997, *Chicago Tribune* travel writer Alan Solomon launched a campaign to locate the best little town in the Midwest and, after six weeks, eight thousand miles, and 139 towns, awarded the title to Bayfield and the Apostle Islands. "This is a place where the lake is sparkling, the beaches clean, the fish abundant and hungry, the golf courses challenging and beautiful, the dining creative, the lighthouses photographable, the bike routes flat, the hiking shaded, the bears reclusive, the sunsets magical and the hours posted at the area's most intriguing saloon are '11 a.m. to whenever.'

"This is Bayfield and the Apostles. This is not a rock group. This is paradise."

Rare is the Bayfield visitor who is unfamiliar with the big blue tent of Big Top Chautauqua.
Photo by Don Albrecht

CORNUCOPIA

(continued from page 125)
Liberty, built in Cornucopia by master boat builder Thomas Jones Sr. in 1934, is undergoing restoration aimed at better sharing the village's maritime glories with visitors.

More about Cornucopia's fishing times, lumber era, and other chapters of the past can be found at the Green Shed Museum adjacent to the beachside park. One of the community's biggest annual events is Cornucopia Day on the second Saturday of each August, but the village's true signature event is the long-running Cornucopia Fish Fry on the first weekend in July; the celebration dates to 1945, when some two hundred pounds of fish donated by commercial fishermen were fried in skillets and served with boiled potatoes, kicking off the tradition that still draws big crowds each year.

Unfortunately for humor's sake, one tradition that did not survive the passage of time was the Cornucopia Yacht Club, begun in 1972 by a local resident named Roger O'Malley. It stood out from other, perhaps stuffier yacht clubs in that members were not required to own a boat. The membership application simply asked, "If you had a boat,

Generations of local and vacationing children have gleefully discovered the natural rock slide in Siskiwit Falls.
WHi Image ID 88053

CORNUCOPIA

what would you name it?" President Gerald Ford was said to have been a member, but the club ended in 1991.

Aside from the post office sign, Cornucopia's most famous feature might be found right across the street in Ehlers General Store, where, in fact, the post office once was housed. Herman Ehlers opened it in 1915 as the Flieth-Ehlers Mercantile Company but it eventually became known as Ehlers, a true general store in the old sense. The store is especially popular with the many summer visitors who come to kayak the lake from nearby Meyers Beach in order to explore the sea caves formed by Lake Superior waves over thousands of years.

There are several waterfalls near Cornucopia, including Lost Creek Falls and Siskiwit Falls, where on warm summer days youngsters can be found sliding on the water-slicked rocks while their older minders are content to wade barefoot in the cool waters.

But the warm days go by in a blur, as one historical anecdote from Wisconsin's northernmost post office village reminds us. In 1940, residents voted to change the name of the community to North Pole, Wisconsin, but postal officials—obviously lacking a sense of humor—refused to accept the change.

Probably a good thing, in the end. Wisconsin's Northernmost Pole just doesn't have the same ring.

12 Modern Bayfield Shaped by Artists' Hands

Jerry and Mary Phillips, both music teachers from Madison, made their first long drive up the spine of Wisconsin to visit Bayfield in 1969. Their first impression was of a dormant little community, though one blessed by a marvelous setting.

"It was sleepy," Jerry Phillips recalled decades later. "Obviously it wasn't that sleepy, because obviously we wouldn't have fallen in love with it. But it was pretty quiet."

It only stood to reason. The decline of commercial fishing in the 1960s, as with the demise of lumbering and quarrying earlier, had left the little city on the lake reeling—no pun intended—once again. As had happened more than once in the past, a natural resource that had served the city and its residents so well had largely been exhausted, adding to the city's history of good times and times not so good.

Sport fishing continued, but not at a level that created many jobs. The national park was still in the future; sailing on Lake Superior was just a niche activity, not at all like the popular pastime it would become; and many who could no longer make a living on the lake were moving away in search of dependable work.

But unlike those other finite resources that had served the city so well until suddenly they were gone, one of the region's most powerful natural assets was mostly untapped and, if nurtured and cared for properly, would be able to serve as the economic engine for the community going forward.

Then, as now, Bayfield possessed an enchanting setting on the greatest of all the Great Lakes.

"All the beauty that is there now was there [then], of course," Jerry said. "It was an amazing kind of special jewel that hadn't been discovered yet." But, he said, for Bayfield's own sake it needed to be found. "There was just no other option. There was tourism. That was what it had to be. I think everybody just felt it's got to be tourism.

Gil Larsen, born in Bayfield in 1898, contributed much to Bayfield's history through his decades of photographs of nature, the lake, and daily life in his hometown. He was an ardent conservation advocate, and today the Gil Larsen Hiking Trail honors his memory. Photo courtesy of the Bayfield Heritage Association, 80-2-639

That's all there was [left]. The town was at its lowest point."

Tourism, of course, had been part of the regional economy for a long time. Bayfield and Madeline Island had gained much attention as a haven for hay-fever sufferers, and summer homes and rental cabins had long been fixtures on Madeline Island. Sport fishing had brought many visitors to test their luck and skills on the waters of Lake Superior, and of course the railroads had made their own contributions to tourism by building hotels nearly a century earlier. But tourism at the end of the 1960s and early 1970s was small in scale compared to what it would become, and as it turned out Jerry and Mary Phillips were significant contributors to its emergence as an economic force in Bayfield.

After visiting a few summers in a row, in 1973 they bought a large Victorian home on Rittenhouse Avenue to serve as their summer "cottage." Of course it was not really a cottage in the usual sense; it was a five-thousand-square-foot mansion that was in urgent need of a thorough renovation, but it was available for less than a traditional cottage would have cost anywhere closer to their home in Madison. Jerry Phillips said they paid $35,000 for the home, fully furnished and with a bottle of champagne waiting for them in the refrigerator.

A year later the oil embargo raised the cost of gasoline to get to Bayfield and heating oil to warm their still-drafty home, so to make ends meet they hung out a shingle and started renting their many bedrooms to other tourists for $8 to $12 a night. Thus was born what would become the legendary Rittenhouse Inn, one of the very first bed-and-breakfast inns in Wisconsin—and, with its hillside setting, giant flower baskets, and wrap-around porch, what would soon be one of Bayfield's most photographed buildings.

After two years of operating the inn during summers only, they left Madison and their jobs behind, opened a restaurant at the inn, and became full-time innkeepers. They would go on to become mentors to the next generation of bed-and-breakfast owners across Wisconsin and beyond, offering classes on how to get started in the business and, more important, how to survive it, and eventually expanded their own offerings to include the Chateau Boutin, the elegant 1908 Victorian Queen Anne that overlooks the busy ferry landing and lakefront.

In the 1960s, Bob Eckels founded a pottery studio in Bayfield. His success helped draw other artists and crafters to the area. Today, his daughter Dede Eckels runs the business.
Photo courtesy of Deanna Eckels

Still, those early years were difficult, in part because tourism was still a nascent industry in Bayfield and also because the season was so short. "It was July and August," Phillips said. "Then September disappeared and in October you had Apple Festival. Then the streets rolled up for the winter."

But help was on the way. The creation of the Apostle Islands National Lakeshore would begin to draw more visitors to the region, and as sailing became increasingly popular, more well-heeled boaters began spending summer vacations in the area. At the same time, the exodus of local residents in the post-fishing years meant homes and commercial buildings in Bayfield were available at bargain prices, and many of those who were attracted were artists who began to draw even more visitors with their creativity.

There had been artists in earlier years, including local photographer Gil Larsen and painters John Black and Bessie Nourse, whose regionally recognized work has been featured in exhibits at the Bayfield Heritage Association. But the artists who began making their presence felt in Bayfield in the 1970s were attempting to make their art commercially successful, and one of the godfathers of the movement would become one of the biggest names in the local art scene.

Bob Eckels, who had been head of the art department at Ashland's Northland College for a number of years, and his partner Glenn Nelson had started a pottery business, the Pot Shop, on Ashland's waterfront in the early 1960s. After two years of so-so success, they decided Bayfield might be a better place to be potters, said Bob's daughter Deanna, or Dede, Eckels.

So, said Dede, "They literally picked up the building, put it on a flatbed and brought it up here. And Bob said it was the best thing that ever happened. I think he had the insight, the foresight, to know that Bayfield was going to become the crown jewel of the state of Wisconsin." Dede went on to become an artist, her father's partner, and his eventual successor in the business that remains one of the city's most prominent today.

There were few craft artists in Wisconsin at the time, but Bob Eckels, who at first spent only summers in Bayfield, helped change that by creating an apprentice program, modeled after European systems in which aspiring artists could learn by working with a recognized master. His first apprentice was Karlyn Holman, who would go on to open a popular gallery and studio in Washburn and who would in turn teach many more area artists.

Soon other artists began making their way to the Bayfield peninsula, creating a community whose work began drawing attention to the area—and drawing tourists, as well. When the Eckels family returned to Bayfield for the summer in 1966, the *Bayfield County Press* welcomed them back.

"Whether or not you like 'pots,' it's a feather in Bayfield's cap to have such a fine artist and teacher as Bob Eckels here," the paper said. "Bayfield is gradually taking its place among the art centers in the state."

A metal sculptor from Illinois, Harold Kerr, moved to Bayfield with his family in 1969 and opened a studio and gallery in a small building facing the water, where his son Brian still operates Kerr Studio and Gallery. Today that site, adjacent to the busy ferry comings and goings and situated on one of the city's busiest pedestrian streets, would be recognized as having that bit of real estate gold known as location, location, location.

But not then. "Oh, it was affordable," Brian Kerr recalled. "The real estate broker that my father talked to said, 'Oh, you don't want that property, it's a tear-down.' Even the real estate people didn't have a clue about waterfront property in Bayfield."

The waterfront then, of course, did not at all resemble the waterfront vacationers find today. One resident who moved to Bayfield in the 1970s remembers it as still

Bob Eckels shows apprentice Kevin Caufield the correct way to trim and finish a pot. Eckels, formerly head of the art department at Northland College, established a pottery apprentice program at his studio.

Photo courtesy of Deanna Eckels

Bayfield's Festival of the Arts showcases the work of both local and visiting artists and helps to bolster the community's reputation as a place of and for artists. Local painter France Austin Miller captured its look in one of her popular watercolors.

Watercolor courtesy of France Austin Miller

very much a working-class city. But much of the evidence was of work that had gone away, from the icehouse once used for packing fish to empty herring shacks and the cannery once used to process the produce of area growers. At the same time, those ghosts of old enterprises spoke of the opportunity—and the need—for something new to emerge.

The number of studios and businesses attempting to appeal to tourists continued to grow—an art-glass store, painters, an artist who worked with leather, and more. And just as auto dealers like to be located near other auto dealers to increase traffic, the artists began to generate their own traffic, inspired by the picturesque place they had found to make art for tourists attracted by the same beauty.

"Bayfield, Wis., is pretty as its artists' pictures," a Minneapolis newspaper declared in 1972. "It's the harbor, the hillside town, the green and hilly countryside, the sea gulls, the variety of boats coming and going, the inn and motels commanding views of the lake, the interesting array of 22 Apostle Islands offshore, the lakeside pavilion, the little

A demonstration by the Eckels Pottery studio at the Bayfield arts festival shows the Raku process, originally an ancient Korean practice, wherein earth, leaves, feathers, and other objects are used to give the pottery a weathered, earthy feel.
Photo by Grandon Harris

pavilion park, the Pier restaurant, the boating, the swimming, the island camping. It all adds up, and then there's the feedback. The tourists attract each other and attract artists and the artists attract tourists."

If that sounds a little too chicken-egg-chicken, there's this simpler explanation from Mary Rice, artist, philanthropist, community booster, and widely acknowledged "queen of Bayfield."

"There's always been artistic creativity around here, in one way or another. I think it was the lake that did it," she said. "Gitchee Gumee did most of it."

Rice, whose family fortune came from the Andersen Window Company, had known of Bayfield's appeal from her family's long summer presence on Sand Island. She remembers spending weeks on the island in summer, where her mother and friends, accompanied by their own cook, would spend time making art. Later, she was herself a frequent visitor to Bayfield before moving to the community and settling in the historic and elegant Knight House, which she proceeded to double in size and fill with all manner of art and life.

She was also a foodie long before the term caught on in recent years. In St. Paul, she had helped start a gourmet cooking school. In Bayfield, she opened Maggie's, the hot-pink restaurant on Manypenny Avenue, and decorated it with eclectic art and photos, a working train set above the bar, and flamingos in all sizes but just one color—pink. Two years later she opened the Clubhouse, a fine dining restaurant on Madeline Island, and several years after that added breakfast to her menu by opening the Egg Toss in Bayfield.

After seventeen years, Rice closed the Clubhouse and brought fine dining back to the mainland by creating Wild Rice, which has won high praise from critics for both its food and architecture and which, in its very name, describes Bayfield's queen as well.

Today the arts continue to serve as Bayfield's calling card. In addition to the many professional artists who live and work in the region, many retirees who have moved to the Bayfield peninsula take art classes and present their own work at shows or in local galleries. Master artists, including painters, jewelry makers, and potters, continue to offer training and classes to other aspiring artists. The Chequamegon Bay Arts Council, based in Washburn, supports art in the region by hosting visual-art exhibits and awarding grants to local artists and organizations. Each summer the Bayfield Festival of the Arts, held the last weekend in July, features the work of nearly a hundred artists from throughout the Midwest and draws thousands of visitors to Memorial Park on the waterfront.

France Austin Miller, a watercolorist known for her paintings of the lake, the islands, boats, lighthouses, and other local scenes, said that as long as there continue to be visitors who want to take a little piece of Bayfield home when they leave, artists will

Painter Tonja Sell displays her talents at the Bayfield Artists Guild.

Photo by Grandon Harris

organizations, and in 2011 Bayfield received the Governor's Tourism Stewardship Award for its exceptional community-wide commitment to sustainability.

That blended focus on preserving Bayfield's history and heritage while at the same time continuing to be a destination that meets the wishes of tens of thousands of visitors annually can often be a balancing act. Many want the city to retain its traditional New England–style look, with church steeples and historic Victorian homes dominating the view from departing ferries as they have for a century or more. Others see hope in development, which seldom fails to raise the eyebrows of the leave-well-enough-alone set. Even as more retirees find their way to the state's northern tip, drawn by its lack of crowds, beautiful scenery, and creative spirit, others worry about declining numbers of families with children. The tourist season now runs well past July and August through September and October, and even cold-weather activities ranging from sled dog races to skiing at Mount Ashwabay to ice fishing on frozen Chequamegon Bay have made winter more than something that must be endured until spring comes again.

Who knows what Admiral Bayfield would think if he could come again today? He never envisioned a town at all, let alone one that would carry his name for centuries forward, even into big-city newspapers like the *Chicago Tribune*, whose writer declared Henry Bayfield's namesake city the "best little town in the Midwest." He can't tell us, of course, but it is tempting to think he would be mightily impressed.

Maybe it didn't turn out to challenge Chicago for greatness, as its early boosters suggested. But on a fine summer day when the berries are ripe and the sun is warm, or on an autumn evening when a full moon rises slowly over Madeline Island and shines its golden smile across the glittering water, no one here will think that a loss.

For More on Bayfield History

This book has provided a broad overview of the history of Bayfield and the Apostle Islands region, but those with an appetite for more can find it at a number of sites.

The Bayfield Heritage Association, 30 N. Broad Street, would be the envy of many cities of considerably greater size. The building includes a museum with changing exhibits on Bayfield life and history, along with a new research and educational facility named for one of the city's most influential founding fathers, R. D. Pike. The museum offers informational programs, summer history lectures, tours, and seminars and should be any curious visitor's first stop. www.Bayfieldheritage.org.

The handsome Bayfield Carnegie Library, 37 N. Broad Street, is in itself a nice bit of local history. In 1857, not long after the city's founding, a library was established as a free reading room. Just after the turn of the next century, philanthropist Andrew Carnegie donated $10,000 for a new library, which led to the construction of the Greek Revival–style building, with columns of locally quarried brownstone, still in use today. Included in its collection of books, magazines, videos, and other materials are a number of volumes about the area. Also available are many videotaped interviews completed in recent years with older residents of Bayfield, whose memories of life along the lake offer true first-person histories of the city and its many transitions. www.bayfieldlibrary.org.

The Madeline Island Museum, operated by the Wisconsin Historical Society, is located a short walk from the ferry landing in La Pointe and offers a thorough and entertaining look at early island history and development. The museum was built by putting together four historic structures, including the last remaining building from the American Fur Company site that dates to 1835. The museum's many artifacts range from Native American and early fur trade and missionary days to later times such as the era of

Benton-Banai, Edward. *The Mishomis Book: The Voice of the Ojibwe.* Saint Paul, MN: Indian Country Press, 1979.

Burnham, Guy M. *The Lake Superior Country in History and in Story.* Ashland, WI: Paradigm Press, 1996.

Busch, Jane C. *People and Places: A Human History of the Apostle Islands.* Omaha, NE: National Park Service, 2008.

Carlson, Mary E. *The Sawmill Community at Roy's Point, 1893–1920.* Bayfield, WI: printed by author, 2009.

Chapple, John. "Bayfield Is Hit By Flood; First Hand Story." *Ashland Daily Press,* July 17, 1942.

Chapple, John C. "'Herring Boom' at Bayfield on Lake Superior." *Wisconsin Magazine of History* 30 (September 1946): 31–38.

Crowley, Kate, and Mike Link. *Apostle Islands National Lakeshore.* Stillwater, MN: Voyageur Press, 1988.

Dahl, Frederick H. *Diary of a Norwegian Fisherman, the Collected Diaries of Frederick A. Hansen.* Jacksonville, FL: Paramount Press, 1989.

Duncanson, Michael. *A Guide to the Apostle Islands and the Bayfield Peninsula.* Cartographic Institute, 1976.

Feldman, James W. *Rewilding the Apostle Islands.* Seattle: University of Washington Press, 2011.

Fifield, Sam. "Beautiful Isles of Chequamegon." *Ashland Weekly Press,* December 21, 1895.

Goc, Michael J., ed. *On the Rock: The History of Madeline Island Told through Its Families.* La Pointe, WI: Madeline Island Historical Preservation Assn. and New Past Press, 1997.

Gould, Whitney, and Stephen Wittman. *Brownstone and Bargeboard: A Guide to Bayfield's Historic Architecture.* Madison: University of Wisconsin Sea Grant Institute, 1998.

Holland, F. Ross Jr. *Great American Lighthouses.* Washington, DC: Preservation Press, 1994.

Holzhueter, John O. *Madeline Island and the Chequamegon Region.* Madison: State Historical Society of Wisconsin, 1974.

Jordahl, Harold C. Jr., with Annie L. Booth. *Environmental Politics and the Creation of a Dream: Establishing the Apostle Islands National Lakeshore.* Madison: University of Wisconsin Press, 2011.

Jordahl, Harold C. Jr., with Annie L. Booth, Kathleen Lidfors, and Carl Liller. *A Unique Collection of Islands: The Influence of History, Politics, Policy, and Planning on the Establishment of the Apostle Islands National Lakeshore.* Madison: Department of Urban and Regional Planning, University of Wisconsin Extension, 1994.

Knight, Eleanor. *Tales of Bayfield Pioneers: A History of Bayfield.* Bayfield, WI: Beedlow Media, 2008.

Larson, Lars E. *Chequamegon Bay and Its Communities.* 3 vols. Whitewater, WI: published by author, 2005–2008.

Loew, Patty. *Indian Nations of Wisconsin: Histories of Endurance and Renewal.* Madison: Wisconsin Historical Society Press, 2001.

Mackreth, Bob. www.bobmackreth.com/scrapbook/hermit.htm.

Norrgard, Chantal. "From Berries to Orchards: Tracing the History of Berrying and Economic Transformation among Lake Superior Chippewa." *American Indian Quarterly* 33, no. 1 (Winter 2009): 33–61.

Nuhfer, Edward B., and Mary P. Dalles. *A Guidebook to the Geology of Lake Superior's Apostle Islands National Lakeshore.* Fort Washington, PA: Eastern National, 2004.

Rasmussen, Charlie Otto. *Ojibwe Journeys: Treaties, Sandy Lake & the Waabanong Run,* Odanah, WI: Great Lakes Fish and Wildlife Commission Press, 2003.

Rennicke, Jeff, and Layne Kennedy. *Jewels on the Water: Lake Superior's Apostle Islands.* Bayfield, WI: Friends of the Apostle Islands National Lakeshore, 2005.

Ross, Hamilton Nelson. *La Pointe: Village Outpost.* 2nd ed. Madison: Wisconsin Historical Society Press, 2000.

Solomon, Alan. "After 6 Weeks, 8,000 Miles and 139 Towns, This Is the Place." *Chicago Tribune,* August 3, 1997.

The Story of Bayfield County, Wisconsin: Its Agricultural and Cultural Advantages. Bayfield County, WI: Bayfield County Board of Supervisors, 1930. Available in the Wisconsin Historical Society pamphlet collection.

Strzok, Dave. *A Visitor's Guide to the Apostle Islands National Lakeshore.* Bayfield, WI: published by author, 1981.

Twining, Charles. "The Apostle Islands and the Lumbering Frontier." *Wisconsin Magazine of History* 66 (Spring 1983): 205–220.

"The Ultimate Summer," *Sailing World,* June 2010.

The author interviewed the following individuals whose quotes are used in this book: Larry Balber, Dede Eckels, Marty Greunke, Fritz Hauser, Sally Heytens, Brian Kerr, Bob Mackreth, France Austin Miller, Julian Nelson, Jerry Phillips, Mary Rice, Jim Vaudreuil.

THE FIRST HOUSE
BUILT BY WHITE MEN IN
WISCONSIN
WAS ERECTED NEAR THIS SPOT BY
RADISSON AND GROSEILLIERS
IN THE FALL OF 1658

Close-up of the Radisson and Groseilliers house historic site marker, commemorating the first house built in Wisconsin by white men. The house was believed to have stood in the vicinity of Ashland at the mouth of Fish Creek where it empties into Chequamegon Bay. WHi Image ID 28810

Index

Photo by Barbara McCann

Dennis McCann spent most of his professional life traveling Wisconsin and the Midwest for the *Milwaukee Journal* and *Milwaukee Journal Sentinel*. A Wisconsin native and graduate of the University of Wisconsin–Madison, he is the author of four previous books on Wisconsin travel and history, including *Badger Boneyards: The Eternal Rest of the Story* (Wisconsin Historical Society Press, 2010). He and his wife, Barbara, a retired teacher, reside in Bayfield, where nearly every day begins with a superior sunrise.